Preparing Your Children For Goodbye

Preparing Your Children For Goodbye

A Guidebook for Dying Parents

Lori A. Hedderman, M.Ed., L.P.C.

Editing and book design by Les Morgan
Front cover photograph by Tony Hedderman
Back cover portrait by Katia Forero (www.katiaforero.com)

Published with technical assistance by Growth House, Inc.
www.growthhouse.org, 415-863-3045

Cataloging information:

Hedderman, Lori A.
Preparing Your Children for Goodbye: A Guidebook for Dying Parents / Lori A. Hedderman. — 1st Ed.
20.32 x 25.4 cm.
First edition
ISBN-13: 978-1460933480 (paper)
ISBN-10: 1460933486

1. Death—Psychological aspects. 2. Death—Children and death. 3. Death—Teenagers and death. 4. Bereavement—Bereavement in children. 5. Bereavement—Bereavement in adolescence.

[DNLM: 1. Terminal Care. 2. Terminally Ill.]

In March 2009, my friend, Sandy, told me that she had cancer. She was the mother of two young boys. Soon after she shared the news with me, I felt an urgent need to begin this project. I wanted to help her and other parents who were ill to create something to give their children to remember them by, to know the hopes and dreams their parents had for their child's future — to read stories about themselves through their parent's eyes.

I didn't get to give her the first copy as I had hoped. She died on May 18, 2010, at home with her loved ones. I wish I had told her that she was the reason I began writing this book. She lived gracefully with her cancer, and always remained positive. Her courage and positive attitude throughout her illness are something that will remain with me always. Our friendship was short in time, but left a lasting impression upon my heart. She was such an amazing person and I am so blessed to have known her.

TABLE OF CONTENTS

ACKNOWLEDGEMENTS

I would like to acknowledge all those who have contributed to the writing of this book in any way, whether through support, content, editing, and commenting on the many drafts I have written. I wish I could list everyone "first" as they are all important to me. (I also wish I could go on and on about how wonderful those listed below really are.)

This is a book for families and extended families, and my own family comes first in my life. Thank you Tony — my husband, best friend and soul mate — for always supporting everything I do. To my son Connor, you are my greatest joy and I am so proud to be your mom. To my parents, Jerry and Sandi Shaffer, I am blessed to call you "Dad and Mom." My mother, Sandi, a cancer survivor, made a particular contribution by reading two drafts and sharing her personal experiences as a patient facing serious illness. She was also a caregiver when my grandmother was dying of cancer. To Jeffrey D. Shaffer M.Ed., I am lucky to have access to such a fabulous proofreader, and most importantly, I am blessed to have you as my brother.

I have had a lot of help from people who are part of my extended family.

To Jason Gillespie, you have always been a true friend and confidant, who helped me to become the counselor I had always hoped to be. Thank you for your unconditional friendship.

To Missy DalBon M.Ed., my friend and colleague, thank you for finding the time to copyedit a draft. You always amaze me with your ability to manage so many responsibilities and still be such a devoted mom.

To Margaret Spinnenweber B.A., my friend and colleague, thank you for editing an early version of my draft. I hope you know I think the world of you.

To Eric Ziegler and Ron D'Amico, my friends, thank you for reading a draft and giving feedback from the perspective of gay parents.

To Rita Gigliotti, thank you for helping me get started with this project. I have not forgotten your help in thinking through questions for the workbook.

My sincere gratitude also goes to the following wonderful people who were gracious to give freely of their time and talents in reading and commenting on the writings of a stranger.

To Les Morgan, the founder of Growth House, you have been my mentor and guide through the process of bringing this workbook to fruition. Your time, patience, and honesty know no bounds. Thank you for sharing your expertise on end-of-life care and the ins and outs of editing and publishing with me. Finding you was no coincidence. Mere words cannot express my gratitude.

To Rev. Keith Knauf, for reading a draft and giving helpful feedback on how life review can be done with hospice patients. Keith is the Director of Pastoral Care Services at the California Medical Facility at Vacaville, California, the site of the first prison hospice in the world. He did not expect that his email message to me would wind up being published, but I am grateful that he allowed us to use it as a Foreword.

To Nancy Jaicks Alexander, for her deep insight into how people approach the end of their lives. Nancy was a member of Elisabeth Kübler-Ross' international teaching and workshop staff. She and her late husband, Robert Evans Alexander, helped to co-found the first prison hospice in the world, at Vacaville, California. Nancy has trained hundreds of hospice volunteers.

To Janice Lynch Schuster, co-author of *The Common Sense Guide to Improving Palliative Care* and *Improving Care for the End of Life*, thank you for conducting a detailed professional review of the content. I truly admire your passion and devotion to your calling as an advocate for improving end-of-life care.

To Viki Kind, M.A., author of *The Caregiver's Path to Compassionate Decision Making*, thank you for conducting a detailed professional review of the book's content and tone. Your work with healthcare professionals, patients, and their families on how to make end-of-life care a compassionate, respectful process has been inspiring to me.

To Susan W. Reynolds, author of *Room for Change: Practical Ideas for Reviving After Loss*, thank you for your helpful suggestions to improve the content of an early draft. Your words of encouragement helped me realize I could really do this project.

To Michael M. Wirth, thanks for making me aware of current research in how doing a life review can be comforting for hospice patients.[1]

To Jim Gebbie, thanks for reading a draft of the workbook and giving me ideas on how it could be used by adult children to interview their elderly parents.

---

[1] Harvey Max Chochinov, Thomas Hack, Thomas Hassard, Linda J. Kristjanson, Susan McClement, Mike Harlos. "Dignity Therapy: A Novel Psychotherapeutic Intervention for Patients Near the End of Life", *Journal of Clinical Oncology*, Vol. 23, No 24 (August 20), 2005: pp. 5520-5525.

FOREWORD BY REV. KEITH KNAUF

Lori,

I feel very honored to be able to preview your book. These are my observations based upon my thirty years of experiences as a pastor and chaplain.

My first thought is personal. I have been actively involved in the lives of over 1,000 individuals and their families as they face death. About 600 of these individuals and their families were prisoners. It has been such a privilege to be there for them at such an intimate time. I made the striking realization quite early in my ministry that I knew more people in heaven than I knew on the earth. Your book brought a flood of these memories back to my conscious mind. I want to thank you for the recall of these memories. I consider them to be very precious.

My second thought is also personal. Your focus on children brought to my mind a dear woman in my church who came to me for counsel. She was 35 years of age and realized she had not dealt with the death of her grandmother. Her grandmother died when she was seven years old. Her parents and other family members wanted to shield the reality of her grandmother's death from her. She did not hold this against them knowing they meant well. However, she remembered wanting to be included in the family talks and in the funeral service. She came up with the idea of assembling a "Memory Book" honoring her grandmother's life. She interviewed many family members and gathered many pictures. I was honored to help her assemble the book.

It is important to treat each hospice patient as an individual. Some want to leave a written legacy for their family. The way the idea of "legacy" is presented in your book is almost exactly what we do in our hospice. The life review workbook could make a wonderful stand-alone booklet for dying patients.

I offer our hospice inmate-patients a writing tablet to use for writing down their thoughts. They write through their pain and through the effects of their analgesics. Some write a kind of diary for their children. Some write words of advice and wisdom for their children. They write about their regrets, what life directions they would change if they could. Some encourage their children to take different life paths than they took. They encourage their children to stay in school and make something of their lives. They all ask their children to forgive them for not being there for them. They also assure them of their love and affection.

I have also seen where our patients want to leave a legacy of artwork, drawings, or craft for specific family members. Our hospice walls are adorned with the artwork of our patients. Some write songs for their families. It is amazing what talent our inmate hospice patients have displayed. They often want to leave this part of themselves to their family and friends. I encourage the families to display these items at funeral and memorial services in memory of their loved one.

One topic that is important for dying patients is the subject of hope. Hope is important. What gives us hope? What are the beliefs, ideals and events that give people the hope they need in their life? What gives them hope now as they face the end of their lives?

Just some thoughts from an old, worn-out chaplain. Thank you for the blessing I received in reading your work.

Rev. Keith Knauf
Director of Pastoral Care
The Robert Evans Alexander Hospice
California Medical Facility

PREFACE

In my calling as a middle school counselor, I often work with grieving students. I remember a time at the beginning of my career when I felt helpless in offering comfort. I knew that saying, "I'm sorry" and offering a hug weren't enough. They needed more. As my experience grew, I learned how to recognize each student's specific needs. I gained a new understanding of the differences between how adults and children grieve. I learned how to talk effectively to parents and address their grief as well.

Perhaps the most important lesson that I have learned from my kids is that life moves on — with or without you. Their adaptability and courage have often moved me to tears. They have always amazed me with the hope and courage they have shown in the face of terrible losses. Your family will get through this difficult time.

This book began as a memory book for my friend, Sandy. It quickly evolved to include advice and information to help you better understand how your children may show grief and how you can reach out to them. I hope that you will find some comfort and guidance throughout the pages, and that your child will feel your love as they read your writings.

Lori Hedderman

INTRODUCTION

This book is a supportive guidebook for parents who are terminally ill. My goal is to help guide you and your children through a difficult time. (I will interchange the pronouns "he" and "she" when referring to your children.) If you have received a grim prognosis, one of your biggest fears may be leaving your children behind. As a result, many questions run through your mind. "Will they be as strong as they will need to be? If they are young, will they remember me?"

Your most important role as a parent is raising your child. All along, you are attempting to impart into them your values, as well as teach them the skills that they will need to be successful as they grow into adulthood. No parent expects to leave a child to journey through life without his or her direct guidance. As that day approaches, and you begin to accept that you will not have the time that you thought you would, the pressure mounts to prepare your child for the future.

If you have picked up this workbook, you have been working through conflicting and confusing feelings. You may have thought, "I'm too young," "I'm too healthy, this can't be happening to me," or "This is a mistake, they must have confused someone else's test results with mine." Perhaps you have refused to discuss any details of your illness, put off doctor's appointments, or continued to do things that you had been told you shouldn't.

You are now ready to begin writing your legacy. It is my hope that this book will help you to capture many of the memories you wish to share with your child and leave an essence of who you really are as a person. Your children will be able to read your legacy many times over as they grow. In the future, they will see you from an adult perspective of their own. It will be good for you to work through these pages, and good for your children to receive the information and thoughts you decide to share. If you have more than one child, you can easily duplicate pages so that each child may have their own copy.

Everyone's life is complex, balancing family and friends, work and leisure. All families are unique, and you may have issues with family members that are deep rooted and complicated. We often try to shield our children from the truth of some situations. As parents, we do not have to, nor should we, bare our souls to our children or tell them every family secret. They may not be capable of understanding some things, and sometimes there is no need for them to know. Sometimes things are better left unsaid. If you feel uncomfortable sharing some memories and feelings with your children, you are not required to. The decision is always yours.

This book is divided into three parts:

- **Part One**, "Living Your Life While Being a Patient", covers end-of-life issues that you will need to consider. This includes arranging for the future by completing advance care directives, writing a will, and planning memorial arrangements. This part also discusses sources for outside help.

- **Part Two**, "Children and How They Grieve", gives you information about how children cope with death and grief. It will guide you through talking to your child about your illness, offer guidance as to when and how to tell your children that you are dying, and explain how children may express their grief.

- **Part Three**, "Leaving Your Legacy Through Life Review", will guide you in leaving behind a written legacy for the people you love. I define a "legacy" as anything that is handed down from an ancestor. One way to define your legacy can be through your writings to those that you love.

At the end of the book, you will see a Bibliography and a list of "Places to Turn To for Help".

WAYS TO USE THIS BOOK

You may use this book in any way you like. As you progress through the sections, you may find yourself feeling overwhelmed with emotion and uncertain as to how you should answer certain questions. This is a normal part of the process. Give yourself the time you need to reach a point of clarity. After collecting your thoughts, continue.

The process of looking back over your life and thinking about what has mattered most to you is a natural part of facing death. There is a formal discipline called "Life Review" in which people are encouraged to discuss and write down aspects of their past. This process, which is also called "reminiscence", can be an important part of working with older people in general.

The Life Review workbook included in this book is specifically designed for use by parents of children and teenagers. It includes questions tailored to help you consider issues relating to your children, as well as more general questions that will trigger memories about other parts of your life. This Life Review process can be used by anyone who is interested in thinking about their own past, even if they do not have children. There are several good books about life review and reminiscence therapy that you can read if you want to go into this subject more deeply.[2]

You can use the workbook on your own or with someone else. It's a nice activity for two people to do together using a conversational approach. If you are finding it difficult to work through these activities alone or if you are struggling with the physical aspect of completing them, you may choose to have another person, such as a friend or some other loved one, assist you. They may read the questions to you and transcribe your answers into the book. They might also help by asking you to clarify your answers in order to achieve more detail. Perhaps your children are old enough to help you and participate themselves.

> "The ideal companion is one to whom you can reveal yourself totally and yet be loved for what you are, not for what you pretend to be."
>
> — Christopher Isherwood

Writing can be tiring. The physical act of writing may require that you sit up. As you get sicker, your ability to write may decline. If you are too weak or too tired to write, you can make audio or video recordings. If you keep a recorder handy, you can work on your stories whenever you want to.

If you do choose to make recordings to share with your children, they will be able to hear your voice, see your face, and feel your presence as they listen to the words meant specifically for them. For very young children, you can record yourself reading books to them. The books you select could be from your collection of childhood favorites as well as from recent favorites that your children enjoy. Your video may also contain clips of you and your children interacting, reading, playing,

---

[2] Barbara Haight's *The Handbook of Structured Life Review* (Health Professions Press, 2007) gives an introduction to life review using a handbook format. Jeff and Christina Garland's (2001) *Life Review In Health and Social Care* (Brunner-Routledge, 2001) covers the use of life review by professionals working in therapeutic settings. Life review can be conducted in group settings, which has an added benefit of promoting social interaction between participants. James Birren and Kathryn Cochran's *Telling the Stories of Life through Guided Autobiography Groups* (The Johns Hopkins University Press, 2001) gives a methodology for group work.

singing, or just enjoying time together. Be creative! Children, especially if they are younger, may not yet understand the purpose behind the recordings. As they grow older, they may cherish this connection to you.

Do not be concerned about your appearance. Your children are not worried about that! They just want you to be yourself so that they see you for who you really are. You will not disappoint them.

Consider recording things that are not covered by this Life Review workbook in a separate notebook or writing tablet. If you like to draw or paint you may want to leave a part of your legacy through your art or craft work that can be given to specific family members.

You may also place pictures that you find particularly meaningful, within this book or in a separate photo album. Consider taking time to explain in writing why you chose particular photographs. You may also want to work on a scrapbook containing photos and memories.

> "I've learned that people will forget what you said, people will forget what you did, but people will never forget how you made them feel."
>
> — Maya Angelou

Letter writing can be a wonderful way to leave a part of your legacy. If you have more than one child, you could write each one of them a personalized, handwritten letter. You may wish to enclose these handwritten letters to communicate your thoughts, feelings, advice, and love. You may choose to write one letter to be given to your child at a later time, or you might decide to write numerous letters to be given during the different developmental stages of your child's life (such as the first days of elementary school, middle school, high school, and college). You may also decide to write a letter to be read to your child as they go through certain significant life events, such as graduation from high school, graduation from college, their first "real" job, marriage, or becoming a parent for the first time. You may choose to give these to your children now or leave them for them to read after your death.

In addition to "final letters", you may benefit by writing regular letters to loved ones. Keep in mind that there is no such thing as a "perfect final message." People will always appreciate letters that express your admiration, gratitude, or love. You may want to ask for or give forgiveness. Expressing your real feelings can be a wonderful tool in relationships.

An adult child could use the conversational method with an elderly parent. It can be an enjoyable way to reminisce about the past and capture memories. This type of conversational approach can be helpful as a tool to use with older people who are having memory problems. Sometimes memories of the distant past are still clear even if the ability to remember recent events is impaired. You can use individual sections of the workbook like a memory game, helping someone to recall things they haven't thought about in years. Exercising the memory is helpful because it keeps the mind active. When using the workbook in this way, you can expect that one memory will bring up another in surprising ways. Enjoy the storytelling! You may even want to record the interviews.

The workbook can be used in hospice settings by hospice volunteers to use with patients who want to reflect on their lives. If someone is too sick to take on a major writing project, the volunteer can ask questions from the workbook to help the person recall anything that they want to have remembered. A volunteer could also work with family members to explain life review ideas and introduce the workbook as something they can use on their own.

Any parent who simply wants to record family history can also use this book. Perhaps you have a high-risk profession in an area such as law enforcement, firefighting, or serve in the military and are concerned about the future. Who hasn't thought, "What if?"

THE ETHICAL WILL

An "ethical will" is a document written, not to give away your material possessions to others, but to reflect on your life and to pass on your values. It can be used to share memories, tell others how much they mean to you, disclose regrets, or ask for or offer the forgiveness you may find difficult doing face-to-face.

Just as each person in the world is unique, so will be his or her ethical will. Some simply write a personal letter to loved ones. Others consider it a work in progress, adding details to a notebook as time goes on. Several good workbooks can help you with writing an ethical will as a gift for your family. I recommend *The Wealth of Your Life* by Susan B. Turnbull[3] and *Ethical Wills* by Barry Baines.[4]

---

[3] Turnbull, Susan B (2005). *The Wealth of Your Life: A Step-by-Step Guide for Creating Your Ethical Will.* Wenham, MA: Benedict Press.

[4] Baines, B. K. (2006). *Ethical Wills*. Cambridge, MA: Da Capo.

Ethical wills usually put most emphasis on a person's values, so they are different from the kind of memory workbook that is included in this book. Our life review workbook includes some values questions, but it also covers personal history and life experiences you want your family to be able to remember.

DEFINING THE TERM "FAMILY"

I define a "family" as the people whom you love and who love you. This may include relatives, friends, community members, or others in your circle of life. Most of us have a friend we are closer to than with many of our relatives. Shouldn't they count as family? Absolutely!

A family is no longer defined only by the term "nuclear", consisting of a married man and woman raising their children. Your family may consist of a single parent (perhaps due to separation, divorce, or a death), the addition of a stepparent (and perhaps their children, creating a blended family), grandparents or another family member raising the child, gay or lesbian parents, and adoptive families. Consider these facts from the United States Census Bureau:[5]

- There are 73.5 million children under the age of eighteen in the United States. Two-thirds of these (68%, less than fifty million) live in a family with two married parents.

- About one in four kids lives in a household with a single female parent, and about one in fourteen children lives in a household with a single male parent.

- Almost one in ten kids (9%) lives with their grandparents or other relatives.

---

[5] Census data from the 2006-2008 American Community Survey was accessed from the American Fact Finder web site (http://factfinder.census.gov) on October 6, 2010. By 2008, the Census Bureau estimated that by the end of 2008 there would be 73.5 million children under the age of eighteen living in United States households. Almost 50 million of these children would live in a family consisting of a married couple; 5 million of these families have a single male head of household, and 18 million have a single female head of household. A further breakdown showed that 89.2% consist of biological, adopted, or stepchildren, 6.5% consist of grandchildren, 2.6% are other relatives, and 1.8% are foster or unrelated children. 6.6% of children live in the presence of other adults in addition to their parent (these other adults are unmarried partners or other unrelated heads of households. Of these unmarried couples, 4.8% were of the opposite sex, and less than 1% were of the same-sex.

- About 2% of children live in foster homes or with unrelated caregivers.

- Almost 7% live with one of their parents and an unrelated and unmarried partner.

- In the United States, gay and lesbian parents are raising four percent of all adopted children and three percent of all foster children.[6]

"The family. We were a strange little band of characters trudging through life sharing diseases and toothpaste, coveting one another's desserts, hiding shampoo, borrowing money, locking each other out of our rooms, inflicting pain and kissing to heal it in the same instant, loving, laughing, defending, and trying to figure out the common thread that bound us all together."

— Erma Bombeck

[6] Gates, G., Badgett, M., Macomber, J., & Chambers, K. "Adoption and Foster Care by Gay and Lesbian Parents in the United States". March 2007. The Williams Institute, UCLA School of Law, in partnership with The Urban Institute. http://www.law.ucla.edu/williamsinstitute/publications/ FinalAdoptionReport.pdf accessed October 22, 2010.

PART ONE: LIVING YOUR LIFE WHILE BEING A PATIENT

More than likely, your life is changing drastically in a very short amount of time. Your physical, spiritual, and emotional well-being is being tested. Relationships may become closer with some people and yet deteriorate with others. You may find comfort in the healing of some relationships, the assurance that you are making plans for your family to be taken care of, or the peace that may develop within you.

You must make decisions in many areas. You must think through legal decisions, financial considerations, end-of-life care, and funeral arrangements. As difficult as the whole process may be, it is essential to begin now.

It is important to remember that you must take care of yourself first. What you need will change from day to day. Hopefully, those around you will extend unconditional love regardless of whether you are happy or sad, cheerful or cranky.

Do not carry this burden on your own. You are not alone. You have the support of your loved ones. You will continue to build upon your support systems and discover new coping skills. Do not be afraid to tell others about your needs. Release your feelings of being a burden if you have not already done so. George Washington Carver, the famous American scientist and educator, once said, "How far you go in life depends on your being tender with the young, compassionate with the aged, sympathetic with the striving, and tolerant of the weak and strong, because someday in life you will have been all of these." There is nothing wrong with reaching out and accepting support.

In addition to developing support systems, it is essential to discover coping skills that work for you. Depending on where you are in your treatment, your ability to be physically active may be limited. If it is not, walking, swimming, and biking may be good ways to relieve stress. Gardening, journaling, reading, and other low-key activities may also interest you. Maybe you already have a hobby or physical activity that you are able to continue to enjoy.

ESTABLISHING SUPPORT SYSTEMS

Well before this time in your life, you have established a support system consisting of family, friends, and groups in which you are active. Your children also benefit from having a support system, both as an extension of yours and on their own.

As your illness progresses, it will be difficult for you to be the main source of support for your children. Accept help from others for yourself and for your family. Bringing together a strong team shows the children that they will be cared for after your death. When you allow others to take on more responsibility for some aspects of the family's well-being, you help build the ongoing support system that your children will need. Letting go in this way might make you feel sad sometimes, but you could also choose to feel proud of how well you are transitioning your children into a safe and secure future.

Don't forget to take the time needed to care for you!

Who makes up your support system? You may have a large circle of people who are with you throughout this difficult time. On the other hand, perhaps you have a small but close-knit circle of supporters. It's important to recognize all of your potential sources of support. Your caregiving network may include anyone who is involved with you and your family. Be open to the love that will come to you from relatives, friends, neighbors, and the other people who are involved in caring for and supporting you and your family during this difficult time.

As a parent, you feel a deep need to take care of your family. The reality is that as your illness progresses it will become harder for you to take care of others. You will need to accept care from them. This can be hard to get used to.

Some people seek support from outside sources, whereas others prefer to stay among family and friends. Many people are very private and do not like to speak to "strangers" about personal matters. These people may feel more comfortable talking to someone they enjoy spending time with such as a close friend or relative. Only you can make this personal choice. Fortunately, many options are available.

There are community organizations, faith groups, and professionals who are dedicated to assisting people in making these difficult decisions. There are many reading materials, websites, and other resources to help you get through what lies ahead.

Many people find great emotional and spiritual hope and support from their choice of faith, whatever it may be. Most professional clergy have received special training from their seminaries and religious schools to equip them with the tools necessary to help them help others through difficult times.[7] These professional clergy should be seen as supportive partners in patient care. Clergy can help families plan funeral and memorial services. They also follow up with families, visiting individuals in their homes both before and after your death. Temples and houses of worship provide families with places where family and friends can gather.

You may wish to find a counselor or therapist who specializes in bereavement and end-of-life care. Others may find solace in community support groups composed of people who are going through many of the same experiences. Support groups are available in most areas, primarily through faith communities, hospitals, community programs, and grief centers. You may also wish to consider online support groups. They can be very helpful and reassuring sources of comfort and information. Please refer to the section entitled "Places to Turn for Help" at the end of this book for more information on how to find help in your area.

Perhaps you, yourself, do not feel the need to seek outside support, but a family member or a friend does. There are many different sources for everyone seeking comfort as they go through this difficult time.

RELATIONSHIPS

It is important to surround yourself with people who are easy to be with and who love you. It is difficult to remain close with negative people even in ordinary circumstances, and it will only be harder to be around them in difficult circumstances.

You may find your relationships with others changing. Those you could rely on in the past may become distant as they struggle with their own fears and emotions. Others, with whom you may not have been close to in the past, might move to the forefront and surprise you with their support and kindness. As they draw closer, they will give you the energy you need to keep going.

There could be many reasons why people react the way they do to your illness. They may or may not be able to express those reasons to you. Whether it is

---

[7] For information about the Association for Clinical Pastoral Education (ACPE), a multicultural, multifaith organization, visit www.acpe.edu.

conscious or not, being with someone who is dying reminds you of your own death. This is an important idea in hospice training. Your impending death may force others to consider their own situation, and that can be scary for them. Even if they handle their own fears well, they may have practical concerns, such as being afraid of saying the wrong thing.

Perhaps you feel that you need to work on healing certain relationships. You may feel that someone has wronged or hurt you in some way, or you may have hurt them. Before you begin, you must realize that you cannot heal all broken relationships. You can only problem-solve for yourself. The only person who can help mend real or perceived relational issues is you. When you try to make something happen that can never be, it can be physically and emotionally draining. That is unhealthy for you. Realize that you can only offer the olive branch — you cannot force another person to take it.

That being said, however, the subject of forgiveness is often misunderstood. Many people believe that when they are wronged, they are somehow punishing the other person by refusing to forgive them. In reality, we are not punishing the other person, but, instead, punishing ourselves. Focusing on our thoughts of anger, resentment, or negativity may affect us emotionally as well as physically.

> Know that many of your relationships
> with others will change

TREATMENT AND CARE PREFERENCES

Depending on your wishes, you must arrange for your end-of-life care. If possible, do you wish to remain at home? Do you wish to be in a hospital? Will hospice be involved? Discuss your options with your doctor to clarify any questions that you may have.

UNDERSTANDING PALLIATIVE CARE AND HOSPICE SERVICES

It's important to understand what the terms "hospice" and "palliative care" mean. Most people have not had enough experience with death and dying to understand all the options they have for their medical care. Once it becomes certain that you can't "defeat" your disease, it is time to change your strategy. Your medical care can put more emphasis on keeping you out of pain and living as fully as possible for as long as life remains.

- **Hospice care** includes palliative care along with other supportive services that are intended to help the entire family. Hospice care is provided by a multidisciplinary team that includes medical care, social work, bereavement support, spiritual care, and volunteer services. Hospice care may be delivered in the home, in medical facilities, and in freestanding hospices. It is generally not provided at the same time as treatments that are meant to cure the disease, but exceptions to this exist for some cases such as children who are terminally ill, and treatments that are primarily palliative in nature.

- **Palliative care** is a type of medical care that focuses on improving the quality of life for patients with serious illness. The goal is to manage pain and reduce symptoms. Palliative care is provided by a team of professionals who work with your primary doctor. It is appropriate at any point in a serious illness and can be provided at the same time as treatments that are meant to cure the disease.

It's wise to ask for a palliative care consultation at any point in dealing with a life-threatening disease. The palliative care team can help you understand all of the options for your care. Looking into hospice alternatives doesn't mean that you are "giving up". It's just smart research. The more you know about your options, the better choices you can make for you and your loved ones.

WHAT ADVANCE CARE PLANNING DOCUMENTS MAY COVER

Do you have certain medical directives that you want followed? "Advance care planning" may include advance directives for healthcare, a "living will", medical orders, and a durable power of attorney for health care. All of these are common names for different kinds of documents used to make decisions for you in the event that you are unable to speak for yourself. The names will vary depending on the state in which you live.

Due to the passing of the Patient Self-Determination Act of 1990, anyone receiving medical care in offices and other such facilities must be asked if they have any of these medical documents in place and they must be offered written information regarding their rights in making decisions about medical care.

Advance care planning has gone through many changes over time. It is your personal decision as to how general or how specific you want your directives to be. According to Bill Colby, who was the attorney for the only right-to-die case that ever went through the U.S. Supreme Court, the best option may be to have a Power of Attorney for Health Care.[8] (Again, this may be called something else depending on your state of residence.) In this document, you name a "proxy" — a specific person — who will have the power to speak on your behalf if you are unable to do so. Be sure that your proxy is someone whom you trust and knows your wishes. Talking to your proxy in advance will help that person make decisions on your behalf based on what you have requested.

These documents may optionally include specific instructions, and if so, these instructions may limit the discretion your proxy has in some situations. Some people try to anticipate the conditions they might find themselves in and list the treatment options they wish for themselves. Other people prefer to focus on simply naming the person they want to make decisions, and leave it up to that person to consider all the facts about a specific situation without tying their hands.

A common use of advance directives is to request that you not receive unwanted medical options that may delay your death by using machines or other treatments. Some of these treatments can make sense if there is the expectation or

---

[8] "Bill Colby on Living Wills", Growth House Radio, 2003, http://www.mywhatever.com/media_files/ growthhouse/podcasts/interviews/bill_colby_22nov2004_32kb.wma, interview of attorney William Colby by Les Morgan, retrieved August 24, 2010.

hope that a patient will recover from a temporary setback. If the person is not likely to recover, they may not have real benefits.[9]

Such treatments may include:

- Use of artificial nutrition given through tubes ("tube feeding")

- Use of artificial intravenous (IV) hydration given through tubes

- Use of a ventilator to enable you to breathe if you are unable to do so on your own

- Use of cardiopulmonary resuscitation (CPR) or use of an automated external defibrillator (AED) to attempt to restart the heart if it has stopped

Some people refuse these types of treatments because they believe that they delay the natural dying process. Life-sustaining treatments like these also can have side effects that may interfere with your physical comfort. Artificially supplied nutrition may prolong the dying process, but may also increase the risk of pneumonia. Hydration may cause the lungs to fill with fluid, which can "drown" the patient.[10] Attempting CPR or using a defibrillator for a person who is terminally ill may also delay the natural process, just as it would by using a ventilator on a person who is already unable to breathe on his or her own with no hope of recovery.

You should clarify your preferences about these things by discussing them with your family and doctor. Remember that you may ask for a consultation with a palliative care specialist or hospice representative in order to understand all of your options. If there is no record of any documentation specifying your wishes or naming someone to speak on your behalf, your loved ones will have to make decisions based upon what they feel you would want. They may not make the same decisions as you would.

If you know that you are approaching death and want to limit the use of some life-sustaining treatments you may ask your doctor to write medical orders to cover some situations in advance. These orders are usually called a DNR ("do not resuscitate") or a DNAR ("do not attempt resuscitation") because in end-of-life

---

[9] Lynn, J., & Harrold, J. (1999). *Handbook for Mortals: Guidance for People Facing Serious Illness.* New York, NY: Oxford University Press, p. 130.

[10] Lynn & Harrold (1999), p.131.

situations the effectiveness of CPR is limited. Some healthcare professionals prefer the term ANR ("allow natural death") for these orders. Another acronym you may hear is POLST, which stands for "Physician Orders for Life-Sustaining Treatment". All of these types of documents have the force of a physician's order, as opposed to an advance directive, which is a statement of your wishes for your care.

The non-profit organization "Aging with Dignity" (www.agingwithdignity.org) has created a national advance directive format that is known as "Five Wishes". This document addresses your personal, emotional, and spiritual needs, as well as desired medical decisions. Almost all states (as well as the District of Columbia) recognize the "Five Wishes" document as meeting legal requirements for an advance directive. The remaining eight states allow the use of Five Wishes as a guide, providing that the individual state's document is attached.

The Five Wishes cover these issues:

1. The person you want to make health care decisions for you if you cannot (Power of Attorney, Proxy, etc.)

2. The kind of medical treatments that you do or do not want (such as life support)

3. How comfortable you wish to be (such as pain management)

4. How you want people to treat you (where you wish to be, such as a home or a hospital)

5. What you want your loved ones to know (such as how to remember you, specifications for memorials, etc.)[11]

> **To get a copy of the Five Wishes document contact Aging With Dignity by calling their toll free number 888-594-7437 (888-5WISHES) or visit www.agingwithdignity.org**

---

[11] "Five Wishes", Aging with Dignity, http://www.agingwithdignity.org/five-wishes.php, retrieved August 30, 2010.

LEGAL AND FINANCIAL PLANNING

Ensuring that you have all the necessary legal documents and any financial issues in order is important for your loved ones as well as for your peace of mind. It is beyond the scope of this book to give legal or financial advice. Family law can be complex, so it's important that you simply do not assume that things will work out as you hope. You may wish to enlist the expertise of a lawyer to compile any necessary documents.

Get competent legal advice if you have questions such as:

- "Who will care for my children?" Knowing that your children will be taken care of is of utmost importance. You must have legal documentation to specify who will be raising your children.

- "How do I write a last will and testament?"

- "Who should be the executor of my estate?"

An estate-planning attorney will be able to answer any questions you may have about your state's laws specific to how to pass on your estate. Legal issues vary from state to state, so you may be surprised at what the law says about who gets what after you die.

An attorney can also help you decide what documents are needed, such as a last will and testament. In most cases, it is a good idea to have a will even if things seem clear. Your instructions need to be written down so nothing is unclear.

For many people, the cost of medical care at the end of life can present serious burdens, even if you have health insurance. Ask yourself:

- Do you have medical insurance that will cover your medical expenses?

- Do you have a cash cushion to draw from if you are unable to work?

- Do you have enough life insurance to cover your family's financial needs?

- How will your family pay for your funeral expenses?

Your directives about financial matters can be recorded in a Durable Power of Attorney for Financial Affairs, a legal document that you can use to appoint a specific person to handle things if you are unable to do so yourself.

Several good workbooks are available to help you bring together all of the financial records, personal information, detailed family history, and funeral instructions that your loved ones will need after you are gone. A good one is *Before It's Too Late* by Emily Oishi and Sue Thompson.[12]

MAKING FUNERAL ARRANGEMENTS

You or your family will need to make decisions about your preferred memorial services. Thinking through your options in advance can take a lot of pressure off your family in the days immediately after your death.

How involved you wish to be in the planning is your choice and depends on your individual level of comfort. Some people wish to be involved in every detail of planning, while others prefer to take little or no part in the decision-making. You may or may not feel up to making any specific plans for your final arrangements. If you decide to do some of the planning yourself, you can use the following planning worksheets to help you think through the questions that your family will face after your death.

There is also the issue of your funeral's expense. The cost of funerals is not specifically covered by life insurance or health insurance policies. If you have life insurance, in most cases, you may use the funds in any way you choose. You may also purchase a funeral insurance policy, though they are often not a very good deal. Unless you already have a specific funeral home that you prefer, it's wise to have someone you trust visit at least two different ones to talk with the staff and get printed price lists. While the funeral industry is sometimes criticized for encouraging unnecessary costs, most individual funeral homes are operated by compassionate people who genuinely want to help families during difficult times.

---

[12] Oishi, E., & Thompson, S. (2008). *Before It's Too Late: Don't Leave Your Loved Ones Unprepared.* Lake Oswego, Oregon: www.before-its-too-late-book.com.

Here are some suggestions on how to reduce funeral costs:[13]

- Cremation is less expensive than burial. The biggest cost of your funeral may be for the cemetery plot or crypt.

- You can lower the cost of many aspects of a funeral by substituting less expensive alternatives for things that the funeral director may suggest.

- If you have no funds at all, and your family is destitute, call your County Coroner for information on public disposition in your area.

- Mortuary Schools offer discounted services (similar to going to a Dental School to have your teeth worked on).

- You may be able to donate your body to a medical school. You must arrange this prior to your death.

- In some circumstances, a burial allowance is available from the Veterans Benefits Administration. For information call 1-800-827-1000 or visit http://www.cem.va.gov/cem/faq.asp on the web.

CHILDREN AND FUNERALS

The first few days following a death are chaotic and overwhelming for everyone involved. Tell young children of the events they need to be prepared for, such as those surrounding the funeral, memorial, or wake that you have instructed your family to have on your behalf.

Do not force your children into doing something they do not want to do. Some children prefer to attend services and others may choose to remain away. Adolescents also need this option. Give them the opportunity to make their own decision. Be careful not to ask leading questions such as, "You don't want to attend the funeral, do you?" Merely give them the information they need to make their own choices. They may or may not change their mind, but hopefully in the future they will not regret attending or staying away from the ceremony because they felt it was what you wanted them to do.

---

[13] For more tips on how to reduce costs see: "What if you can't pay for a funeral?" by Les Morgan, Growth House, Inc., http://growthhouse.typepad.com/les_morgan/2009/01/what-if-you-cant-pay-for-a-funeral.html, retrieved July 16, 2010.

Make them feel needed and useful if they wish to be involved. Many children, teens included, may want to take part by answering the door, answering the phone, taking coats, and so on. Older children may wish to stay behind and watch over the younger children while others attend the ceremony. It is important to include them in a way they are comfortable with, especially if it helps them feel they are doing their part to be involved in the events. Many children make photo collages for the funeral or write letters to their parent to be placed with them.

FUNERAL PLANNING WORKSHEETS

Whom do you want to be in charge of making your funeral arrangements? How can that person be contacted?

Is there a specific funeral home that you wish to use? How can they be contacted?

Have you prepared any detailed instructions for your funeral? Where are those prearrangement instructions located?

How will the funeral expenses be paid? Your plans may change depending on the cost. Have you paid for any of the expenses in advance? Who has the details of those financial arrangements?

Do you want to be buried or cremated? Note any other specific instructions.

☐ Burial in earth

☐ Burial at sea

☐ Entombed in a mausoleum

☐ Cremated

If you wish to be buried or entombed, where would you like that to be?

- Give the name and address of the cemetery you prefer.

- Has the burial plot, crypt, or columbarium niche already been purchased? If so, who has the contract information?

If you wish to be cremated:

- Before the service ☐   After the service ☐

- What would you like to be done with your ashes?

Do you have any personal or religious issues that would affect the handling of your body after death, such as the performance of an autopsy or special religious requirements?

Have you authorized the donation of body parts?   Yes ☐ No ☐

- If yes, where is your Uniform Donor Card located?

- List the names and phone numbers for all people who have been informed of your intentions regarding organ donation:

Have you arranged to donate your body for medical education?

Yes ☐ No ☐

- If yes, give the name of the medical school and the location of the prearranged agreement. You must make arrangements of this type before your death.

Do you want a particular type of memorial service? Give details on any specific preferences you have.

Do you have a specific place in mind to have your ceremony?

Military funeral?   Yes ☐ No ☐

Religious service?   Yes ☐ No ☐

Fraternal ceremony?   Yes ☐ No ☐

Any special music?   Yes ☐ No ☐

Do you want your casket present?   Yes ☐ No ☐

- If yes, do you prefer an ☐ open or ☐ closed casket?

List any special prayers, readings, poems, or letters that you would like to include in the service.

List any specifics such as what clothes or jewelry you wish to wear as well as any other items you want to have with you. Do you want your jewelry or any other items to be removed prior to burial or cremation? You may leave some of these items to your survivors as mementos.

Is there anyone that you would like to give your eulogy or to be your pallbearers?

If you could speak at your own funeral, what would you like to say? Is there a message of hope, thanks, and forgiveness that you would give?

For more information:

Funeral Consumers Alliance, Inc.

http://www.funerals.org

The Funeral Consumers Alliance (FCA) is a federation of nonprofit consumer information societies. Their publications provide funeral planning information with a consumer advocacy perspective.

PART TWO: CHILDREN AND HOW THEY GRIEVE

Many psychologists have studied the ways in which children grieve, and there are many different theories about how grief works. I would like to stay away from using any particular model or "staging" to explain how a child may grieve, and focus instead on common symptoms of grief, the differences between grief and depression, the similarities and differences between adults and children, and some other important considerations such as when to seek professional help.

GRIEF IN GENERAL

Emotions, such as grief and sadness, are appropriate for people at any age. All people, no matter what age, work through grief differently. Your personal way of dealing with grief will be based on your previous experiences and how you were taught to cope with challenges. If you have witnessed how members of your family handled grief in the past, you may try to handle losses in the same way that you perceived them to have done.

There is no specific period of time that a person should grieve. Everyone has his or her own timeline. There is no set amount of time that you or your child will take in moving through these transitions.

Everyone shows a wide range of emotions when grieving. They may respond with feelings such as guilt, anger, worry, fear, shock, relief, hopelessness, or loneliness. They most likely will exhibit common physical symptoms such as crying, loss of appetite, or the disruption of normal sleep patterns. Because some symptoms of grief are very common, they are considered "normal" in the sense that they are "typical", statistically speaking, for a majority of people. A problem with the word "normal" is that some people may have a different reaction that is understandable for them within their own frame of reference, but sometimes hard for other people to recognize as "normal for them" because it is different from their own experience.

Symptoms of "normal" (typical) grief may include:

- Feeling sad

- Feeling angry

- Feeling fearful

- Feeling guilty

- Feeling numb

- Lack of interest in previously enjoyed activities

- Lack of energy

- Weight loss or weight gain

- Loss of appetite

- Sleeping more than before

- Difficulty sleeping

- Physical ailments (i.e. headaches, stomachaches)

- Crying

- Clinginess

- Separation anxiety

Some people experience fewer symptoms than others do, showing a degree of "resilience" that people around them may not understand or identify with. It's important to understand what the terms "resilience" and "durable" mean in the context of grief.

- **Resilience** is a psychological term for a sort of mental toughness that some people have when faced with stressful situations. People who are resilient can "take a licking and keep on ticking" unusually well.

- **Durable** literally means "hard to break". In the context of grief, people who are "durable" aren't just pretending to be O.K., they actually *are* holding up well despite loss.

Children and adults show about the same frequency of resilience in bereavement.[14] People who have this type of durable response are not necessarily just "putting up a good front" and in need of "opening up" in ways that people around them might prefer. They may simply be coping with change in their own way. One study of over 1,400 children found that over two-thirds of them had been exposed to at least one potentially traumatic event (referred to as a "PTE" in the lingo of trauma researchers). Only a small percentage of these children had diagnosable trauma reactions, and the majority of the children in the study showed no signs of any trauma reaction at all.[15]

Recognizing the difference between healthy resilience and unhealthy avoidance can be difficult, but you know your child best. Children and adolescents may try to avoid their grief by pretending that the loss did not happen and that their world is the same as before. They may avoid conversations about the deceased, and places and events that remind them of their loved one. This type of reaction may look like they are coping well, but maybe they aren't. Older children may even try alcohol or other drugs to escape reality.

A person may experience anticipatory grief, which is the feeling of loss before the death actually occurs. A person who is going through this type of grief may show many of the same symptoms as a person who is grieving after the death of a loved one. Even if a person experiences anticipatory grief, this does not mean that their grief after the loss will be any less intense or last for a shorter length of time.

"Disenfranchised" grief can occur if the person who has suffered the loss does not have the sense that people they care about are validating the importance of their loss. Those around them discount their loss, leaving the grieving person unsupported. They may end up feeling shamed by the very people who could be helping them. A person who has had a previous experience with disenfranchised grief may be unwilling to show grief in future losses, or may repeat previous patterns of remaining silent even if the new loss is one that would receive social validation.

---

[14] Bonanno, George A. (2009). *The Other Side of Sadness: What the New Science of Bereavement Tells Us About Life After Loss.* New York: Basic Books. p. 52 cf. note 11.

[15] Bonanno 2009, p. 52, cf. note 13.

FACTORS THAT MAY AFFECT THE GRIEVING PROCESS

Regardless of age, many factors contribute to how any person, adult or child, works through the grieving process. These factors include:

- The closeness of the relationship with those involved.

- Age and developmental level. An elementary-age child has a much different level of understanding of death than a high school student.

- Life experiences.

- Support systems in place.

- Other concurrent stresses that may exist.

- Health (physical and mental). A child who is lower functioning has a much different level of understanding than a child of the same age and of average intelligence.

- Circumstances surrounding the death or anticipation of the event.

- The timeline involved (i.e., a sudden event as compared to a prolonged illness). Someone who has had the opportunity to prepare for an impending loss may react differently than someone who loses a loved one abruptly.

- Previous experiences with death, including the death of pets. A person who has already experienced the death of someone close to them is already familiar with the grieving process as opposed to someone who has not previously dealt with a death.

DEPRESSION AND COMPLICATED GRIEF

When a person is unable to function in his or her everyday life because of overwhelming emotions, this can signal something beyond "normal" grief. Two things to watch for are *depression* and *complicated grief*. Most people who are grieving do not develop these extreme reactions to the loss of a loved one, but you should be aware of the possibility.

DEPRESSION

Major depression is the most dangerous condition that can arise from a loss. Depression can be life threatening. Sometimes depressed people attempt or actually commit suicide.

A person may be having a major depressive disorder if they have a majority of the following symptoms. If these symptoms develop, the person should consider seeking out professional help. Because major depression can look a lot like bereavement, symptoms must be present two months after the death for a therapist to consider diagnosing a client with a Major Depressive Episode.[16]

- Depressed mood most of the time, indicated by feelings of sadness, crying, or feeling empty. (In children and adolescents, this may show up as irritability.)

- Loss of pleasure in normal activities.

- Significant weight loss or weight gain.

- Frequent insomnia.

- Frequent fatigue or low energy.

- Feelings of worthlessness or excessive guilt.

- Difficulty in concentrating or making decisions.

- Frequent thoughts of death, suicidal thoughts, planning for suicide, or actually making an attempt at suicide.

COMPLICATED GRIEF

Complicated or unresolved grief differs from normal grieving in the sense that it interferes with normal functioning or persists with intensity for significantly longer than most people experience. The intensity of the symptoms is greater than

---

[16] American Psychiatric Association. *Diagnostic and Statistical Manual of Mental Disorders (DSM-IV)*, 4th Ed. 1994, p. 327, Diagnostic Code 296xx, "Major Depressive Disorder". Also see: "Other Conditions That May Be a Focus of Clinical Attention", e.g. Bereavement, p. 684, Diagnostic Code V62.82.

in normal grief. Some symptoms of complicated grief are included in this list provided by the American Cancer Society[17]:

- Being unable to accept the death

- Having flashbacks or nightmares

- Severe anger or sadness

- Having a fantasy relationship with the deceased person as if they were present

- Breaking off social contacts

- Complaining of the same physical ailments of the deceased (if the illness was the cause of death)

- Strange or abnormal behaviors

WHEN TO LOOK FOR HELP FROM OUTSIDE SOURCES

Knowing when a child needs more help than you are able to provide can be difficult. Most often, much of what you will experience or will see in your child is to be expected during this time. How long symptoms persist and their intensity are major factors in the difference between a normal reaction to a death and one that may benefit from professional intervention.

The following behaviors, if seen in excess in younger children, may be red flags to warrant speaking to a professional:

- Excessive clinginess

- Oppositional behaviors

- Lowered sense of self-esteem

- Difficulties at school

---

[17] "Major Depression and Complicated Grief", American Cancer Society, http://www.cancer.org/ Treatment/TreatmentsandSideEffects/EmotionalSideEffects/GriefandLoss/coping-with-the-loss-of-a-loved-one-depression-and-complicated-grief, retrieved June 23, 2010.

- Agoraphobia (fear of the outside world or open spaces)

- Lack of memory retention

- Fighting

- Panic attacks

- Fear of abandonment (separation anxiety)

- Intense guilt over the death

- Bedwetting

- Physical symptoms such as weight loss or weight gain

- Sleeping too much or too little

- Nightmares

- Excessive crying

When in doubt, it is better to err on the side of caution. Let someone who is an expert in the field talk with you and your children, and if needed, create a plan of action. Do not hesitate to use your resources — they exist to be used. Another excellent resource (often overlooked) is your pediatrician. He or she can refer you to helpful resources in your area. You will also find many helpful resources in the "Places to Turn for Help" section at the end of this book.

There are many different types of grief support groups. Here are some tips on how to find support near you:[18]

- Hospice care includes bereavement support as part of the total family support, both before and after your death. If you are receiving hospice care, the Bereavement Coordinator for the hospice service you are using can inform your family about support options. Even if you are not receiving hospice services, many hospices offer groups for the public in addition to their clients.

---

[18] Adapted with permission from "How To Find A Grief Group", Growth House, Inc., http://www.growthhouse.org (accessed October 15, 2010).

- Use the Yellow Pages and call hospitals and hospices near you. Ask to speak with the Bereavement Coordinator, Social Worker, or Chaplain's Office to get a local grief referral.

- Call your telephone operator and ask for the numbers for your local mental health association and your local suicide prevention center. Both agencies have good grief referral lists. You do not need to be suicidal to get a grief referral from a suicide prevention center.

- If you are mourning the death of a child, check the national office of The Compassionate Friends (www.compassionatefriends.org) to see if there is a group near you.

GRIEF IN CHILDREN

There are many books on death for children and adolescents (and for you) that you may find helpful. My goal for this section is to give you a brief overview of some key ideas. To learn more, see the "References and Recommended Reading" section, which is organized by age level and grade level.)

Although both adults and children share many of the same feelings and emotions when grieving, there are many differences as to how they exhibit these feelings. When a parent dies, a child's world turns upside down. They are now without a normal routine and have no idea how they are to continue with their own life. Things will not be the same. They are unsure of what the future holds, and quite possibly, who will care for them.

Your child will experience many transitions. They are attempting to make sense of their new world, and just starting to establish a sense of what the new "normal" will be for them. They must reorganize their world in a way that will allow their lives to move forward.

> **Children often show their grief differently than adults**

It is important to make it clear that there is no need to hide grief. Children need to know that they do not need to be ashamed of the magnitude of their love for someone they have lost. Tell them clearly that it is good to have pride in the fact that someone has touched your life so deeply.

Remember to let them be kids. They are not capable of being substitute adults. They are not the man or woman of the house now. They actually need their childhood now more than ever.

At any given moment, a child may seem overwhelmed by his or her grief, only to instantly switch gears and become distracted by something else. This may be upsetting to some adults, as they may think that the child isn't really bothered by the loss or is being selfish. However, this can be a normal reaction for a grieving child.

Children may regress to an earlier stage of their development. A young child who has been toilet trained may suddenly require diapers again; a teenager who doesn't like to be hugged or comforted may become clingy and need constant reassurance.

Children may "regrieve" when life changes significantly for them.[19] Such events may be triggered years after the loss. They do not have to be triggered by sad situations, happy events can trigger these feelings as well. A graduation, a wedding, a move, or even the birth of a child may have this effect.

There are also significant differences in how males and females grieve. Girls are more likely to report problems such as headaches, stomachaches, or other physical symptoms. They are also more concerned for their own safety and that of others. They may dwell on the possibility of an illness, an accident, or any other traumatic experience that could possibly occur to the surviving family or to themselves. Girls are more likely to cry, to express their feelings by talking to others, and hold on to mementos that remind them of the deceased. Boys tend to talk less and display their grief through action. They may act out their grief through episodes of anger and aggressiveness. Of course, this is not to say that girls can't be aggressive, or that boys can't cry and be clingy. Again, each child experiences grief in their own way, regardless of what gender they are.

> They are children. They need to play, to learn, and to grow in their own time.

---

[19] The term "regrieve" is taken from Emswiler, J. P., & Emswiler, M. A. (2000). *Guiding Your Child Through Grief*. New York: Bantam, p.24.

TAKING A CLOSER LOOK AT DEVELOPMENTAL LEVELS

Here are a few items to consider that may help you to understand how children at different developmental stages view death. It is important to remember that a child's age may not be as relevant as where he or she is in their developmental process. Everyone is unique in his or her own understanding of death. You know your child better than anyone else does.

THE YOUNG CHILD (INFANTS TO AGE 5)

Use truthful and age-appropriate language when talking to children of any age. We often use euphemisms when talking about death, but these can confuse young children. Don't use vague explanations about death, especially with younger children, as they may take what you say literally. Of course, you are not going to be able to talk to an infant as you would to a three-year-old since their ability to understand and process language is different.

From birth to around age three, a child's greatest fear is separation. The child may not have a sense of "object permanence" — the understanding that the caregiver has not disappeared forever when he or she simply leaves the room for a minute or that a toy has not disappeared forever when it is simply hidden under a blanket and cannot be seen. From the ages of three to six, a child may continue to have problems understanding the difference between a short absence and a permanent one.

Young children may not grasp the physical aspects of dying. They may view death as reversible or temporary. Cartoon characters can fall off a cliff and in the next scene be perfectly fine. They may believe the person can return, that the person will have the power to see them after death, or may simply be sleeping, able to wake up at any given moment. It is often difficult to explain to young children that the person is not only lying still but also no longer has a heartbeat or the ability to move or breathe. They may be concerned that the deceased is still in pain.

Use real terminology. For example, if young children are told that you will be "going to sleep" or "going away," they may think that you will be able to wake up or come back. Explaining death to your

> ### What you can do:
>
> Explain what it means to die, and that the person cannot return to life. Do not give more information than what the child seeks. Let them guide you with their questions.

children in this manner may also trigger a fear of going to sleep based on the belief that they may not wake up either.

It is important to tell your child that the death is not their fault, and they did not make this happen. Children this age have magical thinking. They may believe that wishing for something can make it so. For example, if children wish that it would stop raining so that they can go outside to play and then rain does stop within the next few minutes, they may think their wish has been granted. They, themselves, made the rain stop. If they have been angry with a parent, they may think that their anger caused the parent to become ill or die.

Young children often act out their grief through play. They may role-play scenes such as a funeral or a wake, or even "play" dead by lying still with their hands folded over their chest. This may help them to make sense of the grief in their lives.

THE SCHOOL AGE CHILD (6 TO ADOLESCENCE)

From the ages of six to around ten, children's understanding of death increases. They are beginning to understand the biological aspects of death, as well as the feelings that are brought on by the grieving process. They know that death is final, but they do not quite understand the concept of mortality.

Do not use euphemisms for death such as "daddy is sleeping." These inaccurate statements can cause an irrational fear of going to sleep.

Be sure to explain to younger children that death is not a punishment for bad behavior. Your loved one did not become ill because they did something wrong.

From the ages of ten to twelve, in addition to the biological and the emotional aspects, children often bring spirituality into the mix. Children may think about the existence of an afterlife and may ask questions about it. They may ask questions such as, "What happens to a person when they die? Do they become a ghost? When you die, will you still be able to watch me play baseball? What happens to your soul when you die?"

Young children are, at times, less verbal than adults when trying to work through their emotions. They are still learning how to verbalize their feelings

What you can do:

Answer your child's questions honestly. If you are comfortable, talk to them about your personal views of spirituality. Keep it simple and answer truthfully.

when expressing themselves. They may be more physical in the way that they exhibit their feelings. They may lash out at others, or, on the other hand, may be loving and affectionate.

THE UNIQUENESS OF ADOLESCENCE

Teens deserve a special section all to themselves. They are no longer children, yet not quite adults. Teenagers are struggling to gain their freedom and independence, and yet need accountability. They push you away one moment, only to turn back to you the next. Their peers are quickly becoming their main source for advice as well as a source for their sense of importance, yet they still need you to set their boundaries. They argue, get angry, throw tantrums, and ten minutes later may be back to hug you and ask for the car keys. Their moods change quickly as they travel along a roller coaster of emotions. Adding the loss of a parent to this already difficult time in their life is like throwing fuel onto a fire. Though they may try harder to push you away, they need you now more than ever.

From the ages of twelve to eighteen, adolescents have a well-developed cognitive understanding of death. Teens, unlike young children, understand the finality and permanency of death. They may have experienced the death of a pet, or even of a loved one, and know that the deceased will not return.

> ### What you can do:
>
> Keep the lines of communication open, and listen to any concerns they have. Be honest concerning your feelings about death as well. They need to know that you are experiencing some of the same feelings as they are. Just making yourself available to them is a positive start.

Unfortunately, invincible thinking is prominent at this time. The adolescent may think, "It can't happen to me." They think that death always happens to someone else. At this age, they are most likely to engage in risky behavior such as speeding, driving under the influence of alcohol or drugs, taking on dares, having unprotected sex, or taking unnecessary risks in sports or activities with peers.

You may see your adolescent behaving as if nothing has changed in their world. They may refuse to discuss any aspects of your illness with you or with anyone else. Do not try to force them into talking about the situation. The harder you push, the harder they will push back. Do not be surprised if they change the subject or leave the room if the topic comes up. Just try to be patient and be available for them when they are ready. Setting boundaries for self-disclosure is part of the process of growing up. The need for personal autonomy and privacy is very strong during adolescence and is a healthy part of becoming an adult. Keep giving the message that you are supportive and available to talk, while respecting boundary-setting behavior.

Their peers are becoming the main place to seek solace and comfort while trying to distance themselves from adults. They are trying to find their own identity, to find who they really are among their peers. Now they must reassess their role within their family. How will the family dynamics change? How will they fit in? What will happen now?

Just as recommended for younger children, it is very important to try to keep a teenager's routine as normal as possible. Encourage them to continue with enjoyable activities, be positive with schoolwork, and hang out with friends. Life must go on.

Because there are many symptoms of grief that can occur in all ages, adolescents show many of the same symptoms as other age levels. Because of the turbulence of adolescence, which they are already experiencing, they are also more likely to:

- Experiment with drugs or alcohol

- Express suicidal thoughts or attempt suicide[20]

- Injure themselves (e.g., cutting)

- Engage in risky behavior (e.g., promiscuity, dares)

- Act overly strong and mature (e.g., modeling adult behavior)

- Suffer from lowered self-esteem

Many teens struggle with these issues. Watch for any change in behavior that may indicate that your child needs to speak with a professional.

---

[20] Suicide is the third leading cause of death among adolescents in the United States. Suicidal thoughts and behaviors are common in adolescence. The CDC's National Youth Risk Behavior Survey found that in 2005, among students in grades 9 through 12, 16.9% seriously considered suicide, 13% planned suicide, and 8.4% attempted suicide. Another study found that 20% to 30% of adolescents think about suicide, 19% in the past year. Range, L. M. (2009). Adolescents and Suicide. In: D. E. Balk, & C. A. Corr, (Eds.), *Adolescent Encounters with Death, Bereavement, and Coping* (pp. 81-93). New York: Springer Publishing Company.

BREAKING THE NEWS TO YOUR CHILDREN

In addition to having many questions of your own, you have the added concern that your children may ask questions that you cannot answer, or you are not ready to answer. This can be an opportunity for instruction on one of life's greatest lessons: learning to effectively process grief.[21]

Although we often feel that our children are too young or too sensitive to process the illness and death of a loved one, children growing up in today's society are more aware of the reality of death than we realize.[22]

Be honest with your children or adolescents. They are very adept at sensing when something is not right in their world. It is better for you to tell them the facts sooner rather than later so that you do not leave it to their imaginations to fill in the blanks. The unknown is often more frightening to children (as well as to adults) than reality. By talking with them and giving realistic, age-appropriate information, you can alleviate unnecessary anxiety.

You need not be overly concerned about hiding your feelings and emotions from the children in your care. They need to know that being brave does not mean that you can't cry. Tears can express many different feelings. They can be a sign of grief, of pain and discomfort, or of relief and joy. When you share your feelings, you give your children a safe place to express their feelings as well.

> "How can I help you to say goodbye? It's okay to hurt, and it's okay to cry. Come let me hold you and I will try. How can I help you to say goodbye?"
>
> — Patty Loveless

---

[21] Shaw, E. (1994). *What to do when a loved one dies: A practical and compassionate guide to dealing with death on life's terms.* Irvine, CA: Dickens, p. 248.

[22] Grollman, E. A. (1990). *Talking about death: A dialogue between parent and child.* Boston: Beacon, p. ix.

I like the "Four T's" approach to helping a grieving child: <u>Talk, Touch, Tears, and Time</u>.[23]

- **<u>Talk:</u>** Remember that "talking" includes a lot of "listening" too.

- **<u>Touch:</u>** Hug your children often. Showing affection aids healing. Some children may become more affectionate. However, if they do not wish to be touched, respect their space and let them know that your arms are always open.

- **<u>Tears:</u>** Do not be afraid to cry in your children's presence. Maybe they will cry right away or not at all. Respect the fact that everyone grieves in his or her own way.

- **<u>Time:</u>** Be patient. It takes time to heal, and everyone moves through deep feelings at a different pace.

Make sure that you are available to talk with your children on an ongoing basis. Talk with them about the changes that are occurring or will occur in your lives. Encourage your children to talk with other family members and caregivers about what they are feeling and thinking. By creating a climate of open communication, you will be able to give support and identify concerns quickly.

It's important that the adults in the family get on the same page about how to talk with the children. Otherwise, the kids may get different stories from different people. If the other adults in your family have a different communication style, or believe different things, talk with them about what you think would be best for the children to know and encourage all of the grown-ups to give consistent messages to the children. This form of open communication may be different from what your family is used to. Cultural differences may also affect the degree of openness within your family.

> ### The Four "T"s
>
> Talk
>
> Touch
>
> Tears
>
> Time

---

[23] "Do's and Don'ts with Grieving Children", Haven of Northern Virginia, Inc. http://www.havenofnova.org/articles/children_in_grief/do_dont_grieving_children.pdf, retrieved July 17, 2010. The "Four T's" have been highlighted in several articles without attribution to an original source.

HAVING THE FIRST CONVERSATION

From an early age, some children seem to understand more than we think they are capable of understanding, while others are slower to understanding death in a way that most children at their age would. It is important to adjust the conversation to your child's particular level.

Find an appropriate time and place to tell your children the news. Choose a setting that will be least likely to upset their routine. For example, never wait until bedtime to tell your children the news. If you do, bedtime may become an anxiety-filled time of the day for your children.

Try to keep the following questions in mind as you contemplate how you will talk to your children.

- Are they immature or lagging socially?

- Are they "wise for their age"?

- Is this the first death that they will experience?

- Has the topic of death previously been discussed?

- Do they have another caregiver to lean on during this difficult time?

You may begin by telling your children that you have something important to discuss, and then explain that you are ill. Be careful to differentiate between being ill with a cold or similar sickness as compared to being ill with a terminal illness. If you do not clarify the difference, younger children may think that if they catch a cold they could die, too. They may think that your illness is contagious. Some people may be afraid to touch you or be in the same room with you if they have irrational fears about catching your illness. The majority of deaths are not caused by communicable diseases, but there are exceptions.

> You may say something like this: "My illness is not like a cold. You cannot catch it. It will not make you or anyone else sick."

It is important to tell your children what is happening to you. Talk to them about the illness itself and what you are doing to live with it. Don't be afraid to tell them how you feel about the process. Name your illness, explain what it is, and begin to tell them what they may expect along the way. You do not have to disclose everything at one time. You may wish to explain certain aspects or treatments as they become more likely.

Answer questions as best you can, and do not pretend to know everything about your specific illness. Admit that you do not know everything about death or the terminal illness you face. Acknowledge when you do not know something, and tell the children that you will seek answers to their questions. You and your children may choose to seek the answers to your questions together.

> ### What you can do:
>
> It is important to continue to comfort very young children and make sure they are held, cuddled, and engaged by the parents as much as possible.

If you are receiving treatment for your illness, talk to your children about how you may feel afterward. You may be extremely tired or nauseous, your hair may fall out, etc. Some kinds of treatments can suppress your immune system. In such cases, you may need to limit contact with other people for a while.

Take into account that children often attune themselves to their parents' needs. If they think that you need them to be strong and pretend that they are fine, they will try to meet your expectations. Adolescents often try to act in this manner. Children may think that if they show their emotions in your presence, it will make things harder for you. Encourage your child to share their feelings with you, but *only if they feel comfortable in doing so.* We often make the mistake of thinking that our children are developing the same coping skills that we have, when, in reality, we may be hindering their ability to work through their grief in their own way.

> You may say something like this: "It's Okay to be sad and cry. I know that it's because you love me so much, and I love you too."

Because children react differently depending on their developmental level, they respond differently to this kind of news. Some children may overload you with questions right away, while others will talk to you when a specific question arises. Most young children live in the present, so your news may be taken in stride until it interferes with the child's "here and now." This should not be seen as callousness. It is normal for children to be egocentric — everything in their world revolves around them! On the other hand, older children often want to ask specific questions about anything from medications to finances. All children need time to process and cope, just as you do.

If discussing your beliefs about the afterlife, do not make it sound too wonderful. Adolescents may consider suicide, in order to join the deceased and relieve their grief. Do not say that God "wants" you to be with Him or "is taking me" to be with Him. Some children may direct their anger toward God for taking their loved one.[24]

The time will come to go through your personal effects. Just as it will be difficult for you to let go of many material possessions, children of all ages may have similar attachments to objects. Try to work together to make decisions about your belongings. You may choose to donate clothing to charity, or there might be specific pieces that hold a special memory for one or both of you.

Keep your expectations realistic and age appropriate. Neither a child nor an adolescent can be a substitute adult, and you do not want to deprive them of their childhood. Avoid telling them that they will become the "man or woman of the house".

SPECIFIC THINGS TO SAY AND NOT SAY

You can set a positive tone for your conversations by becoming aware of some of the expressions you use when discussing illness and death. Noticing these specific phrases can help you reframe thinking. It's also important to consider how people will talk with your child about your death. Here are some ideas for ways to reframe common things people say about death to make them more realistic and supportive of a child's needs:

> You may say something like this: "I'm going to live with this as well as I can so that I can spend as much time with you as possible. My body will get weaker until it just won't work anymore. It's like a machine that finally doesn't work anymore and can't be fixed. When your body stops working completely, it's called dying."

---

[24] Some people don't think there is anything wrong with being angry with God. In some religious traditions, it is considered better to think of God as multifaceted, and able to handle whatever we need to feel at the time.

Instead of saying this:	Consider saying this:
"Your dad passed away." "Your mom is sleeping." "We lost your mom." "Mom has gone away."	"Your mom died."
"Only the good die young." "God took dad to be with him." "Mom was taken to heaven."	"Dying is a natural part of life." "No one is to blame."
"Sometimes when people get sick they don't get well again." "I promise I won't die too."	"Most of the time when people get sick they get well again. Dad's disease was different from what happens to us when we get sick."
"Now you're the man of the house." "Be brave. Boys don't cry."	"You did everything you could." "It's important that we all go on with our own lives. That's what mom would have wanted us to do."
"Don't cry in public."	"It's OK to cry, and you may see me cry too."
"Wouldn't you rather skip going to the funeral home?" "You don't want to go to the funeral, do you?" "We all must go to the funeral together."	"There will be a ceremony to honor mom's life. You can attend if you feel OK about going, but it's also OK for you to stay home or just attend parts of the ceremony if you prefer." "This is what you may see and hear at the service."

LIFE GOES ON

Make sure that your family knows you want them to go on living fully. As they do, things will change in their lives, and they will know that your love will always be with them as they grow and flourish. Show through your example that the world does not stop or slow down after a loss — it continues on with or without you.

You should try to keep routines as "normal" as possible. Children and adolescents need to be with peers and continue attending school, playing sports, and taking part in other important obligations and pastimes. Continue to let your kids be kids! Urge them to continue in their activities. Keep things as familiar and as routine as possible. Encourage them to see and spend time with friends as they normally would.

> It is important to keep a child's routine as "normal" as possible.

At the same time, you are facing the reality that "normal" no longer exists. You must work together toward a new sense of what the "new normal" will be for your family. Adjusting to life without your loved one will take quite some time and the process of grieving can take months or even years.

Be realistic about what you can do. Do not promise that you will be able to go to a school function, a play, a game, and so on, as you do not know what the future holds. You can only tell them that you really want to attend these special occasions with them and that you will do your very best to make it to their events. You may consider having someone video an event if you are unable to attend. You and your child can watch the event together later.

If they have plans to attend a day camp or if you are planning to go on a family vacation, keep those plans if you are still feeling well enough.

Keep changes in routine at a minimum. Although young children are adaptable and are often able to adjust to change better than adults, they still need structure because their routines make them feel safe. They also need frequent breaks and downtime to get away from the crisis and just be a kid. Having a consistent routine helps them. Make sure to stick to the rules. Remain consistent in disciplining your children. They need to know your expectations still apply. Structure and routine are important aspects to maintaining their comfort level.

As you continue to build your support system, your children must build one too. Other people, such as relatives or family friends, will be taking care of your children in the future. They will help support you and your children during your illness and beyond.   Their presence is important for children at all developmental stages.

Talk to your children's teachers and school counselors for support at school. During the week, teachers see your children for more hours of the day than you do. A quiet child may have outbursts, an outgoing child may withdraw, and a child's grades may decline.   Teachers will be aware of any of these changes and can alert you as well as the school counselor.   The counselor's office is a safe place for children to express themselves.   School counselors can also be a source for referrals to outside counselors or agencies, if they are needed.

HOLIDAYS

Holidays, such as Mother's Day and Father's Day, as well as the anniversary of your death, may be difficult times for your child.   Pay attention to any reaction that your child may have, whether in anticipation of the day or the day itself.   Do not assume that your child is struggling and force them to talk about their feelings. Unlike you, they may not even be aware that the day on the calendar is significant!

Think about the last holidays that you will be spending with your family. Will the traditions remain the same?   Will you create new traditions or modify old ones?   Of course, there is simply no way to keep everything as it has been in the past.   Ask your children to help you decide how to celebrate your last holidays with your family.   Attempt to plan for the future so that the "firsts" without you will be easier on the family to bear during holidays, anniversaries, and birthdays.

Many children enjoy hearing stories as a means of comfort.   Write down, film, or record good memories, fun times, and cherished stories.   Perhaps your family may get together to re-live some of those times during the holidays.

SUMMARY OF KEY IDEAS FOR HOW TO COMMUNICATE

- Be simple

- Be direct

- Remember the child's developmental level

- Encourage questions, but don't concentrate on unnecessary details

- Be patient

- Be available

- Be open and honest

- Let your children talk freely and express their feelings

- Don't downplay their concerns

- Share how you feel, and encourage your children to do the same

- Know that it's okay for them to see you cry

- Continue to keep routines as normal as possible

- Turn to others for support and comfort

PART THREE: LEAVING YOUR LEGACY THROUGH LIFE REVIEW

You can use this Life Review workbook to pass on your values and facts about your life that your child may be curious about in the future. The workbook is broken down into five topics:

- You and Your Family

- School Days

- Intimate and Close Relationships

- Parenting

- Telling Your Child's Story

Each topic is divided into smaller activities that should not take very long to complete. You may start at any point and work at random. Choose activities that mean the most to you. If you aren't interested in a certain topic, or a specific activity within, feel free to pass over it. There is no need to go back and complete each one.

> "I never travel without my diary. One should always have something sensational to read in the train."
>
> — Oscar Wilde

1. YOU AND YOUR FAMILY

Take this opportunity to tell your children about your earliest memories of childhood. Tell them about your family members. What it was like growing up? The term "family" as used here includes all of the people who care about you, or whom you care about.

There are nine activities:

- Early Childhood & Family

- Growing Up in Your Neighborhood

- Those Who Helped Raise You

- Others Who Make Up Your Family

- Family Vacations

- Relationships with Family Members

- Beliefs and Faith

- Witnessing Significant Historical Events

- Helping Your Child To Get To Know You

> "You don't choose your family. They are God's gift to you, as you are to them."
>
> — Desmond Tutu

1.1 EARLY CHILDHOOD AND FAMILY

When and where were you born?

Who were the members that made up your family?

Where did you grow up?

What was your childhood home like? (You may want to draw a sketch or blueprint of the layout of the home and the neighborhood)

Did you have your own room or share it with someone? Share your memories of your room — how it looked, what you liked to do, if it was a special place for you.

Did you have any childhood pets?

What were some of your favorite meals that your family had?

> "When you were born, you cried and the world rejoiced. Live your life so that when you die, the world cries and you rejoice."
>
> — White Elk

1.2 GROWING UP IN YOUR NEIGHBORHOOD

How would you describe your neighborhood?

Did you play with any particular neighborhood friends?

What games or activities did you enjoy?

Is there a story that you would like to share about your neighborhood (funny, strange, etc.)

Did you ever move? If so, talk about where and how many times you moved. Was it a local move or a move that took you away from the area you lived in before?

> "I came from a real tough neighborhood.
> I put my hand in cement and felt another hand."
>
> — Rodney Dangerfield

1.3 *THOSE WHO HELPED RAISE YOU*

Who raised you?

If raised by your biological parents, how did they meet? How old were they at the time?

What were their ethnic backgrounds? Were they born in this country or in another one?

What languages were spoken in your home? Were you encouraged to speak more than one language?

What did your parents do for a living?

Did they like their vocations? Were you ever tempted to follow in their footsteps? Why or why not?

Are your parents and important caregivers still alive? If not, when did they die? How did their deaths affect you?

> "Parents can only give good advice or put them on the right paths, but the final forming of a person's character lies in their own hands."
>
> — Anne Frank

1.4 OTHERS WHO MAKE UP YOUR FAMILY

How many brothers and sisters do you have, including stepsiblings? (If you'd like, add names, ages (older or younger), and anything else about them that you would like to share.)

Do any members of your family have a nickname? What is the story behind it?

Who were your cousins and were you close to any of them? What kinds of things did you do for fun?

What about others who were part of the family?

Did you have a favorite person that you felt especially close to? What made them your favorite?

If you were adopted or raised in an extended family setting, what was that like for you?

Is there anything you wish you knew about your family that you haven't been able to find out?

Use this space to share any other thoughts or memories.

> "The most important thing in life is to learn how to give out love, and to let it come in."
>
> — Morrie Schwartz

1.5 FAMILY VACATIONS

If you went on family vacations, where did you go? Whom did you go with?

What are some of the most memorable vacations? What happened that made them so memorable?

Did you have a favorite vacation spot?

What were some of your favorite souvenirs that you remember bringing home? Do you still have any of them?

Is there a vacation that you would have enjoyed taking and never did? Where would you have gone?

"I have found out that there ain't no surer way to find out whether you like people or hate them than to travel with them."

— Mark Twain

1.6 RELATIONSHIPS WITH FAMILY MEMBERS

Who are you most similar to in personality and in what way? (This may require some extra thought).

To whom is your child most similar in personality and in what way?

How were you different from others in your family?

Is there anything you felt you had to keep secret from your family?

What were some words of advice that your parents and caregivers shared that stuck with you?

What do you feel that you may have taken for granted with your parents and caregivers?

What would you have done differently in reference to your family relationships, if anything?

> "We achieve inner health only through forgiveness — the forgiveness not only of others, but also of ourselves."
>
> — Rabbi Joshua Loth Liebman

1.7 BELIEFS AND FAITH

Often, religion and spirituality are very difficult subjects to discuss. However, they are important in many people's lives. You may believe in a higher power, attend a place of worship, have recently found yourself rethinking your beliefs, have recently converted from one belief to another, or may not believe in a higher power at all. Perhaps you are unsure if there is anything to believe in. People often change their perspective on spiritual issues as they go through life. Perhaps your beliefs today are different from those you had earlier. Whatever the case may be, this section will allow you to pass on the things you want your children to know about your feelings on faith, spirituality, and religion.

Were you raised in any particular faith?

Did you attend a specific place of worship?

Did you attend a religious school at any point in your education?

Have your beliefs changed? If so, why, and in what ways?

What are your current beliefs?

Who helped to shape your beliefs?

Have you faced any struggles or opposition due to your beliefs?

> "A person consists of his faith. Whatever is his faith even so is he."
>
> — *Bhagavadgītā* 17.3

1.8: WITNESSING SIGNIFICANT HISTORICAL EVENTS

Take a few moments to write down your personal memories of some of the historical events that you have witnessed throughout your life. Share some events that were significant to you, where you were when you learned of them, how you felt, and the reactions of those around you. Baby Boomers often talk about where they were when Neil Armstrong walked on the moon or the world's reaction to President Kennedy's assassination.

"Four things support the world: the learning of the wise, the justice of the great, the prayers of the good, and the valor of the brave."

— Muhammad

1.9: HELPING YOUR CHILD GET TO KNOW YOU BETTER

Here are a few items that are sometimes overlooked as we often think we already know our loved one's favorite things. Perhaps your favorites have changed from the time you were young. Take a few minutes to write answers regarding your favorites from then and now.

Favorite	In the past	Now
Foods		
TV shows		
Movies		
School subjects		
Songs		
Animals		
Cartoon characters		
Candy		
Best days ever		
Sports teams		
Colors		
Sports to play		

Favorite	In the past	Now
Hobbies		
Games		
Books		
Vacations		
Actors/Actresses		
Holiday		
Season		
Comic books		
Gifts		
Birthday (if celebrated)		
Cars		
Family traditions		

2. SCHOOL

Whether you were a big fan of school, hated every moment, or fell somewhere in between, your children probably have many questions about your experiences. Social time with friends, classes, crushes, sports, and the prom — all can make for good stories.

Be honest about your memories. If middle school gave you some of the worst memories of your life, talk about it! Kids know that life at school could not have been perfect for you, and it's guaranteed that it will not be perfect for them. Sometimes, it is nice to know you are not the only one who feels a certain way.

Whatever your decisions regarding your education, tell your story. If you went right into a job out of high school, feel free to write about that. Maybe you did not graduate from high school. Maybe you are happy with the decisions you made for your future. Maybe you have regrets. You may have wanted to attend another school after graduating high school, but could not. Perhaps you did not have the funds or the grades to apply, had your sights on another path, or had other extenuating circumstances.

There are eight activities:

- Preschool, Kindergarten, and Elementary School

- Middle School Academics

- Middle School Social Life

- High School Academics

- High School Social Life

- High School — Looking Back

- Higher Education

- Higher Education — Social Life

> "The difference between school and life? In school, you're taught a lesson and then given a test. In life, you're given a test that teaches you a lesson."
>
> — Tom Bodett

2.1 PRESCHOOL, KINDERGARTEN, AND ELEMENTARY SCHOOL

What are some of your earliest memories of school?

Did you walk to school, ride in a car, or ride a bus?

Who were your best friends? Are you still friends with any of them?

What were your favorite classes? Why?

Who were your favorite teachers? Why?

Did you have any favorite games to play during recess? What were they? Did you play any sports or belong to any clubs (i.e., Cub Scouts or Brownies)?

How would other children (or your teachers) have described you (i.e., quiet, shy, outgoing, class clown, smart, teacher's pet)?

Did you ever get into trouble? If so, give an example.

Did you win any awards?

> "It takes courage to grow up and become who you really are."
>
> — e. e. cummings

2.2 MIDDLE SCHOOL ACADEMICS

Did you attend a public or a private school?

What was the name of the school(s) that you attended?

What was the school mascot?

Was middle school a positive experience for you? Why?

Did you have a favorite teacher? If so, what made them special?

What were your favorite subjects? Why?

What subjects were the most difficult for you? Why?

Did any middle school teachers give you advice that has stuck with you over the years? If so, what was it?

"At fourteen you don't need sickness or death for tragedy."

— Jessamyn West

2.3 MIDDLE SCHOOL SOCIAL LIFE

Did you play any sports or belong to any clubs or organizations?

Did you play any musical instruments? Were you in the chorus, band, or orchestra? Were you in any school plays?

What did you do for fun on the weekends with friends?

Who was your best friend?

Which social group did you most strongly identify with?

In what ways were you different from your friends? How so? (e.g., religion, culture, sexual orientation)?

What kind of relationship did you have with your parents?

Do you remember any embarrassing or funny moments?

What were some of the difficulties you experienced during middle school (i.e., with friends)?

> "I failed to make the chess team because of my height."
>
> — Woody Allen

2.4 HIGH SCHOOL ACADEMICS

What was the name of the school(s) that you attended?

What was the school mascot?

Was high school a positive experience for you? Why or why not?

What were your favorite classes? Why?

Who were your favorite teachers? Why?

What subjects were the most difficult for you? Why?

Did you ever get into any trouble during high school?

Did you win any honors or awards?

Did you graduate? Do you remember your graduation ceremony?

"Education is not the filling of a pail, but the lighting of a fire."

— William Butler Yeats

2.5 HIGH SCHOOL SOCIAL LIFE

Did you hang out with the same friends during high school that you had during middle school? How did your relationships change?

Did you play any sports or belong to any clubs or organizations?

Did you play any musical instruments? Were you in the chorus, band, or orchestra? Were you in any school plays?

What did you do for fun on the weekends with friends?

Who taught you how to drive? What was your first car?

Did you have positive role models for close personal relationships?

Did you have a steady boyfriend or girlfriend? Did you date often? If you are gay or lesbian, when did you come out? What was that like for you?

Were you quiet, popular, or the class clown?

Do you have any yearbooks from high school?

> "True terror is to wake up one morning and discover that your high school class is running the country."
>
> — Kurt Vonnegut, Jr.

2.6 HIGH SCHOOL — LOOKING BACK

Did any high school teachers give you advice that has stuck with you over the years? If so, what was it?

Did you know what you wanted to do after graduation? Did you plan to attend college?

Did your relationship with your parents improve, stay the same, or worsen during this time?

Do you feel that you chose good friends and made good decisions?

Do you regret any choices that you made during this time of your life?

Do you still keep in touch with any of your high school friends?

"The trick is growing up without growing old."

— Casey Stengel

2.7 HIGHER EDUCATION

Did you attend college, university, or a trade school? Was this your first choice? If not, where did you really want to go?

What did you major in? Did you ever change your major?

Why did you choose that particular area of study?

Did you complete your program? What degree(s) did you earn?

Did you live at home, in a dormitory, an apartment, or somewhere else?

How did you pay for school (i.e., loans, grants, scholarships, parents, work)?

What were your classes and your professors like?

Did you graduate with any honors, awards, etc.?

"The only thing that interferes with my learning is my education."

— Albert Einstein

2.8 HIGHER EDUCATION — SOCIAL LIFE

Did you play any sports or belong to any fraternities, sororities, clubs, or organizations?

Describe some of your best friends. Do you still keep in contact with anyone?

Were you active in any political or social movements?

Did your attitudes about spirituality and religion change during those years?

What are a few of your best memories?

Did you stay in the same career field after graduation?

Would you have done anything differently? If so, what?

"Even if you are on the right track, you'll get run over if you just sit there."

— Will Rogers

3. ADULT LIFE

We all spend time outside of our own homes. Interactions with other people often take place at the office, and many people consider their careers to be a very important part of who they are. People who serve in the military have their entire lives affected by experiences they have there. Being active in social groups and political efforts brings meaning and focus to many people.

There are three sections:

- Work

- Military

- Social and Political

> "Yesterday is history, tomorrow is a mystery. And today? Today is a gift. That's why we call it the present."
>
> — Babatunde Olatunji

3.1 WORK

Was work or a career important to you? Why or why not?

What was your first job? How did you like it?

Did you work at any jobs that you particularly enjoyed? What did you like about those jobs?

Who was your best boss? What did you learn from that person about life?

Did you ever start your own business? What was that like?

How well did you balance work with personal life? Were there ever times when they were out of balance?

If you were a homemaker, how did you see yourself as part of the family support system?

> "To love what you do and feel that it matters — how could anything be more fun?"
>
> — Katharine Graham

3.2 MILITARY

Did you serve in the military? If so, share some of your memories about your time in the service. What led you to enter the military? Did you serve in an active war zone?

Were you a Conscientious Objector?[25] If so, share some memories about your alternate service. What led you to become a Conscientious Objector?

Did you want to serve in the military but could not do so for some reason?

Regardless of your own military service, did having friends or family in the military affect you in some way?

> "Without heroes, we are all plain people, and don't know how far we can go.
>
> — Bernard Malamud

---

[25] In some countries, including the United States, a Conscientious Objector (CO) is someone who refuses to perform military service on grounds of conscience or religion. As a substitute for military service COs may be assigned to perform alternate service in a civilian role.

3.3 SOCIAL AND POLITICAL

One person can make a difference. How have you made a difference to someone else, either within your own family or within the community?

Have you ever been active in any political or social organizations?

Have you ever served as a volunteer for a non-profit or community organization? What did you learn about life from volunteering?

Over the years, have there been times when you felt particularly connected to, or disconnected from, the community in which you lived?

What are some of your most important views on social or political matters?

Is there any advice you would give your children about involvement with their community?

"Let us live happily then, not hating those who hate us. Among men who hate us, let us live free from hatred."

— Dhammapada 197

4. INTIMATE AND CLOSE RELATIONSHIPS

One of the subjects that children often want to know more about is that of their parents' personal lives, such as their crushes, relationships, and dating.

I hope that your love story involves a "happily ever after." Even if it has not turned out the way you hoped it would, you may still leave good memories for your children concerning both the joys and the difficulties of relationships.

There are many different situations in which people find themselves with a partner. What works for one couple may not work for another. Most likely, they live together, although some do live apart. They may be married, or remain unmarried, either by choice or by limitations placed upon them by religious restrictions or laws in their state, such as limitations on same-sex marriage.

There are three activities in this section:

- Early Relationships

- Thoughts Regarding Relationships

- Thoughts Regarding Commitment

"Just because someone doesn't love you the way you want them to doesn't mean they don't love you with all they have."

— Unknown

4.1 EARLY RELATIONSHIPS

Who was your first crush? Your first kiss? How did it turn out?

What qualities did you see in the person who interested you?

When and where did you go on your first real date? How did you meet?

If an important relationship ended, what were some of the conflicts or differences that made it hard for you to work things out?

What are your opinions about the appropriate age to date and curfew times?

"That's why they call them crushes. If they were easy, they'd call them something else."

— from the movie Sixteen Candles

4.2 THOUGHTS REGARDING RELATIONSHIPS

Is there a certain period of time that you feel a couple should be together before they make a lifelong commitment?

Is there a certain period of time you feel a couple should be together before they have a child?

What are some of the joys of being in a relationship with someone?

What are some of your favorite memories of your relationship with your partner?

What are some of your partner's qualities that complement yours?

"You can tell more about a person by what he says about others than you can by what others say about him."

— Leo Aikman

4.3 THOUGHTS REGARDING LOVING RELATIONSHIPS

There are many ways to form loving relationships. What were the most important loving relationships you have had?

What are your views on commitment?

Was the idea of marriage important to you?

What are your views on living together, in lieu of, or before marriage?

Have you ever been separated or divorced?

Do you wish or expect that your children will marry some day? What advice would you give your children for their wedding day?

Do any of your children not want to marry? How do you feel about that?

"Chains do not hold a marriage together. It is threads, hundreds of tiny threads, which sew people together through the years."

— Simone Signoret

5. PARENTING

One of the most important (and often one of the most difficult) tasks in the world is being a parent. As you well know, parenting is more than just creating children. You must also instill character in them and raise them to be happy and healthy. We sometimes raise our children similar to how we were raised. We may remember the things we did not like about our upbringing and try to change those things to better suit our own parenting style. There are times when we get it right, and there are times when we don't. Sometimes we make minor mistakes, and sometimes they are larger than we wish to admit.

One thing that we all have in common (and this certainly applies to you or you would not be working through this book) is that we love our children. They make us angry, but we still love them. They make us cry, but we still love them. They disappoint us, but we still love them. They break our hearts, but we still love them.

There are two activities in this section:

- Personal Experiences

- Parenting Advice

> "While we try to teach our children all about life, our children teach us what life is all about."
>
> — Angela Schwindt

5.1 EXPERIENCES AS A PARENT

Do you feel that you took anything about your parents for granted?

What have you done differently in raising your children than your parents did when they raised you?

Did you feel ready to be a parent?

What are a few of your favorite things about being a parent?

What are a few of the most difficult things about being a parent?

What are a few things that you have learned about yourself after becoming a parent?

"The most important thing that parents can teach their children is how to get along without them."

— Frank A. Clark

5.2 PARENTING WISDOM

Is there a certain age that a person should be before they are "ready" to become a parent?

What do you feel are the most important morals and values that you should teach to your children?

What are a few of your hopes and dreams for your children?

What parenting advice do you have for your children?

If you could tell your future grandchildren one thing about the world you grew up in what would it be?

If you could give advice to them to help them negotiate through life, what would it be?

"Our character is what we do when we think no one is looking."

— H. Jackson Brown Jr.

6. TELLING YOUR CHILD'S STORY

All kids, no matter what age, seem to love hearing stories about themselves when they were younger. "Tell me the story about when I was born," or "Tell me about when I was a baby," are common statements that you may hear. Use this section to relive the wonderful (and sometimes embarrassing) memories and stories you have about them. If you have more than one child, you may want to photocopy these blank pages to complete for each one.

There are four activities:

- Beginning Your Child's Story

- Recording Your Child's Favorites

- Sharing Additional Memories of Your Child

- Sharing Advice

"Before you were conceived I wanted you. Before you were born I loved you. Before you were here an hour I would die for you. This is the miracle of life."

— Maureen Hawkins

6.1 BEGINNING YOUR CHILD'S STORY

Tell about your child's birth. Tell the story about when you first laid eyes on your child.

What was it like to bring your child home for the first time? Who visited your child during the first few days at home?

What was your child's room like?

How well did (or didn't) your child sleep through the night (as a newborn)?

How quickly did everyone settle into a routine?

What was your child like as a baby (i.e., smiley, quiet, fussy, sleepy, playful)?

If your child was adopted, talk about how and why you decided to adopt and the circumstances of the adoption.

If you did not meet your child until after infancy, what was their personality like at the beginning of your relationship?

"A new baby is like the beginning of all things — wonder, hope, a dream of possibilities."

— Eda J. Le Shan

6.2 RECORDING YOUR CHILD'S FAVORITES

Your child's favorite:

Foods:

Toys:

Games:

Books:

Songs:

Gifts:

Traditions:

Pets:

TV Programs:

> "Too many people grow up. That's the real trouble with the world, too many people grow up. They forget."
>
> — Walt Disney

6.3 SHARING ADDITIONAL MEMORIES OF YOUR CHILD

Something funny or cute your child did early on:

Your memories of your child's first day of school:

Special times spent with your child when he or she was younger:

What are some of the qualities and characteristics you see in your children?

"A baby is God's opinion that the world should go on."

— Carl Sandburg

6.4 SHARING ADVICE

Parents are always prone to giving advice. Take a few minutes to write down a few words of advice or wisdom for your children on friendships, dating, marriage, family, or anything else that comes to mind.

"There are some people that if they don't know, you can't tell 'em."

— Louis Armstrong

6.5 HOPE

When life got tough, what kept you going?

What are the beliefs, ideals and events that gave you hope when you needed it in your life?

What gives you hope now as you face the end of your life?

"Although the world is full of suffering, it is also full of the overcoming of it."

— Helen Keller

BIBLIOGRAPHY

DEATH AND DYING

Kramer, H., & Kramer, K. (1993). *Conversations at midnight: Coming to terms with dying and death.* New York: Morrow.

Levine, S. (1997). A Year To Live: *How to Live This Year as If It Were Your Last.* New York: Crown Publishers, Inc.

Lynn, J., & Harrold, J. (1999). *Handbook for Mortals: Guidance for People Facing Serious Illness.* New York, NY: Oxford University Press. (An online version of the full text of this book is available at www.growthhouse.org)

Oishi, E., & Thompson, S. (2008). *Before It's Too Late: Don't Leave Your Loved Ones Unprepared.* Lake Oswego, Oregon: www.before-its-too-late-book.com.

Pausch, R. (2008). *The Last Lecture.* New York: Hyperion.

Polce-Lynch, M. (2006). *Nothing left unsaid: Creating a healing legacy with final words and letters.* New York: Marlowe.

Shaw, E. (1994). *What to do when a loved one dies: A practical and compassionate guide to dealing with death on life's terms.* Irvine, CA: Dickens.

ADVANCE CARE PLANNING

Doukas, D. J., & Reichel, W. (2007). *Planning for Uncertainty: Living Wills and Other Advance Directives for You and Your Family.* Second edition. Baltimore: The Johns Hopkins University Press.

Kind, V. (2010). *The Caregiver's Path to Compassionate Decision Making.* Austin, Texas: Greenleaf Book Group Press.

Kingsbury, L. (2009). *People Planning Ahead: A Guide to Communicating Healthcare and End-of-Life Wishes.* Washington, D.C.: American Association on Intellectual and Developmental Disabilities.

LIFE REVIEW AND REMINISCENCE THERAPY

Birren, J., & Cochran, K. (2001). *Telling the Stories of Life through Guided Autobiography Groups.* The Johns Hopkins University Press.

An introduction to life review using a handbook format.

Garland, J., & Garland, C. (2001). *Life Review In Health and Social Care: A Practitioners Guide.* East Sussex: Brunner-Routledge.

Covers the use of life review by professionals working in therapeutic settings.

Haight, B. (2007). *The Handbook of Structured Life Review.* Health Professions Press.

Life review can be conducted in group settings, which has an added benefit of promoting social interaction between participants.

ETHICAL WILLS

Baines, B. K. (2006). *Ethical Wills.* Cambridge, MA: Da Capo.

Turnbull, Susan B. (2005). *The Wealth of Your Life: A Step-by-Step Guide for Creating Your Ethical Will.* Wenham, MA: Benedict Press.

GRIEF BOOKS FOR ADULTS

American Psychiatric Association (1994). *Diagnostic and Statistical Manual of Mental Disorders*, 4th ed. Washington, DC: American Psychiatric Association.

D. E. Balk, & C. A. Corr, (Eds.). (2010). *Adolescent Encounters with Death, Bereavement, and Coping* (pp. 81-93). New York: Springer Publishing Company.

Bonanno, George A. (2009). *The Other Side of Sadness: What the New Science of Bereavement Tells Us About Life After Loss.* New York: Basic Books.

The Dougy Center (n.d.). *What About the Kids? Understanding Their Needs in Funeral Planning and Services.* Portland, Oregon.

Emswiler, J. P., & Emswiler, M. A. (2000). *Guiding Your Child Through Grief.* New York: Bantam.

Goldman, L. (1999). *Life and loss: A guide to help grieving children.* New York: Brunner/Mazel.

Greenwall-Lewis, P., & Lippman, J. G. (2004). *Helping children cope with the death of a parent: A guide for the first year.* Westport, CT: Praeger.

Grollman, E. A. (1990). *Talking about death: A dialogue between parent and child.* Third Edition. Boston: Beacon Press.

Grollman, E. A. (1996). *Bereaved Children and Teens: A Support Guide for Parents and Professionals.* Boston: Beacon Press.

Huntley, T. H. (2002). *Helping children grieve: When someone they love dies.* Minneapolis, MN: Augsburg.

Kroen, W. C. (1996). *Helping Children Cope with the Loss of a Loved One: A Guide for Grownups.* Minneapolis, MN: Free Spirit.

McWhorter, G. (2003). *Healing Activities for Children in Grief: Activities suitable for support groups with grieving children, preteens and teens.* TX: Gay McWhorter.

Reynolds, S. W. (2010). *Room for Change: Practical Ideas for Reviving After Loss.* Austin, Texas: Revival Publishing.

Worden, J. W. (1996). *Children and grief: When a parent dies.* New York: Guilford.

GRIEF BOOKS FOR YOUNG PEOPLE, BY AGE AND GRADE LEVEL

The following books are written for use by young people. For younger children, it may help if you sit with the child and read with them or to them. Some books for very young children use a lot of pictures to tell the story.

EARLY CHILDHOOD (PRESCHOOL)

Frisbie Juneau, B. (1988). *Sad but OK: My Daddy Died Today — A child's view of death.* Nevada City, NV: Blue Dolphin.

> A nine-year-old tells of dealing with her father's terminal illness and his approaching death. Her questions are answered honestly by her parents. Through reading about another child's experiences, such as visiting the funeral home and cemetery, your children can see how they can be involved in the end-of-life process.

McLaughlin, K. (2001). *The Memory Box.* Omaha, NE: Centering.

> This book tells the story of a young boy whose grandfather has died. He talks about all the things that he and his Grandpa did together and how he misses him. He creates a memory box out of Grandpa's tackle box and places items within it that remind him of the special times that they shared.

AGES 4-12 (GRADES K–6)

Boulden, J., & Boulden, J. (1994). *Goodbye Forever Activity Book.* Weaverville, CA: Boulden.

> This activity and coloring book explains in simple terms the concept of death as a natural process. It includes sections on saying good-bye, burial, the ways death is different from sleep, and accepting feelings.

Brehm, M., & Wenzlaff, R. (2007). *Get rid of the hurt: A reproducible workbook for kids experiencing loss.* Warminster, PA: MarCo Products.

> This book helps children understand why people grieve and includes many pages for children to write or draw their thoughts and feelings.

Buscaglia, L. (1982). *The Fall of Freddie the Leaf: A story of life for all ages.* Thorofare, NJ: Slack.

> Freddie the Leaf learns about the cycle of life as he and his friends go through the seasons. It is a wonderful allegory for the process of life and death.

Curry, Casey (2003). I Remember You Today: An interactive picturebook for children dealing with loss and grief. Annapolis, MD: The Annapolis Publishing Company.

Jaffe, Suzan E. (2003). *For the Grieving Child: An Activities Manual.* Charleston, MA: Acme Bookbinding Co., Inc.

> An activity book for grieving children. Some of the activities could be used with very young children if an adult guides them. There is a fairly brief introduction to grief written for adults.

Kaplow, J., & Pincus, D. (2007). *Samantha Jane's Missing Smile: A story about coping with the loss of a parent.* Washington, DC: Magination.

> Samantha Jane's father has died, and she no longer feels like smiling. A kind neighbor notices her struggle and asks her about her missing smile. She opens up about her feelings and thoughts of the fear that she and her mother will never be happy again. She realizes through talking with her neighbor, and with her mother, that it is okay to be happy even though her father cannot be with her to enjoy life together.

Silverman, J. (1999). *Help Me Say Goodbye: Activities for helping kids cope when a special person dies.* Minneapolis, MN: Fairview.

This activity book helps children express their grief through art by way of drawing and writing their responses to open-ended questions pertaining to death and bereavement.

Stickney, D. (2004). *Water bugs & dragonflies: Explaining death to young children.* Cleveland, OH: Pilgrim.

This book for small children addresses their questions about what lies beyond the grave. The author uses the metaphor of dragonfly larvae, which live below the surface of the water, and of their change into adult dragonflies, which fly above the surface, to illustrate the notion of someone going out of our sight to a wonderful place. They cannot come back to tell us about it; instead, we have to wait for our time to go to them.

AGES 13-14 (GRADES 7-8)

Heegard, M. (1988). *When Someone Very Special Dies: Children can learn to cope with grief.* Minneapolis, MN: Woodland.

This book is intended to help children through various levels of grief using writing and drawing. It is a valuable tool, especially for those who still have issues with verbally expressing their grief.

McLellan-Marino, Julie (2005). *We Love Each Other: An activity book for grieving children.* Bloomington, IN: Trafford Publishing.

An activity workbook for grieving kids aged 9 or 10 and older. The format is "hands-on" and encourages the child to draw, paste photos, and write stories as part of a supportive process of remembering the person who died, particularly a mom or dad.

Schwiebert, P., & Deklyen, C. (2005). *Tear Soup.* Portland, OR: Grief Watch.

Grandy is a wise woman who has just experienced the death of someone she loves. She begins to make tear soup (an allegory for the grieving process), which is made differently by each cook who makes it. This wonderful book explains the ways that each person grieves in his or her own way and timeframe.

AGES 15-18 (HIGH SCHOOL)

Grollman, E. (1993). *Straight Talk About Death for Teenagers: How to cope with losing someone you love.* Boston: Beacon Press.

Intended to be read by teenagers, this book covers practical coping strategies for everyday life. The format is easy to read, using large type and lots of white space to make the text less overwhelming.

Hughes, L. (2005). *You are not alone: Teens talk about life after the loss of a parent.* New York: Scholastic Paperbacks.

This book lets teens know that they do not have to feel alone and there is help available. The book opens with the author's story of losing both of her parents by the age of 12. Readers talk about what it is like to go through the process of grieving and dealing with life without a parent.

PLACES TO TURN TO FOR HELP

Aging With Dignity

> 888-594-7437 (888-5WISHES, toll-free)
>
> http://www.agingwithdignity.org
>
> Provides the "Five Wishes" advance care directive documents to help you express how you want to be treated if you are seriously ill and unable to speak for yourself.

American Association of Pastoral Counselors

> 703-385-6967
>
> http://www.aapc.org
>
> This is a membership organization, which has over 1600 pastoral counselors listed for referral. If you wish to receive counseling from a mental health professional with a seminary degree who can guide you spiritually, please refer to this site's directory.

American Cancer Society

> 1-800-ACS-2345
>
> http://www.cancer.org
>
> The goal of the American Cancer Society is to prevent cancer, save lives, and diminish suffering from cancer. The ACS has a comprehensive site index to find information on practically any topic pertaining to cancer, as well as links to support services and programs near you.

American Counseling Association

> http://www.counseling.org
>
> The American Counseling Association is dedicated to the growth and enhancement of the counseling profession by providing continuing education, publications, research, and other information that assists counselors in expanding their knowledge and expertise. You can use their search engine called "Counselorfind" to locate counselors' names, locations, and specific areas of practice using a list compiled by the National Board of Certified Counselors.

American Psychological Association (APA)

> 800-374-2721
>
> 202-336-5500
>
> http://www.apa.org
>
> The APA website has a link to its Psychologist Locator. By typing in your local information, such as zip code, you will be given a list of psychologists in your area.

Association for Clinical Pastoral Education (ACPE)

> 404-320-1472
>
> www.acpe.edu
>
> ACPE is a multicultural, multifaith organization devoted to providing education and improving the quality of ministry and pastoral care offered by spiritual caregivers of all faiths through the clinical educational methods of Clinical Pastoral Education.

Children's Grief Education Association (CGEA)

> 303-722-2319
>
> http://www.childgrief.org
>
> CGEA is a nonprofit organization dedicated to serving the needs of grieving children and families by providing education and support to those who serve them. Their web site contains helpful information and links to other informative sites.

The Compassionate Friends

> http://www.compassionatefriends.org
>
> 877-969-0010 (toll-free)
>
> The Compassionate Friends offers a nationwide support network for bereaved families after the death of a child. It has more than 625 chapters with locations in all 50 states.

The Dougy Center for Grieving Children and Families

> http://www.dougy.org
>
> This site lists over 500 centers that provide grief counseling and services. On the website, you can type in your city, state, zip code, or the name of a particular center in your area.

The Family Caregiver Alliance: National Center on Caregiving

> 415-434-3388 or 800 445-8106
>
> http://www.caregiver.org
>
> The Family Caregiver Alliance has a website for those who are providing care for seriously ill or elderly family members. It offers programs at national, state and local levels to support and sustain caregivers. Informational sections contain tips and advice, as well as suggestions for further resources.

Funeral Consumers Alliance, Inc. (FCA)

> 800-765-0107
>
> http://www.funerals.org
>
> FCA is a federation of nonprofit consumer information societies protecting a consumer's right to choose a meaningful and affordable funeral. FCA publications provide funeral planning information with a consumer advocacy perspective.

Growth House, Inc.

> 415-863-3045
>
> http://www.growthhouse.org
>
> Growth House distributes information about end-of-life care for both professionals and the general public. With over 4,000 pages of educational material on death, dying, hospice, palliative care, grief, and other related topics, this organization has one of the most comprehensive sites on the Internet. It has an online bookstore that includes most of the books listed in the bibliography of this book.

National Cancer Institute

> NCI Public Inquiries Office
>
> 1-800-422-6237
>
> http://www.cancer.gov
>
> The NCI site contains information about practically everything about the topic of cancer, including a section on coping with loss and bereavement.

National Hospice and Palliative Care Organization (NHPCO)

> 703-837-1500
>
> http://www.nhpco.org/
>
> NHPCO is the largest nonprofit membership organization representing hospice and palliative care programs and professionals in the United States. Their mission is to improve end-of-life care and help provide access to hospice care for those who are terminally ill and their loved ones. Their web site includes a search feature that can help you locate a hospice or palliative care program by state or city in the United States.

ABOUT THE AUTHOR

Lori A. Hedderman, M.Ed., N.C.C., L.P.C., is a certified school counselor who works with children and their families in the public school system. Her work brings her into contact with many students who are losing a parent or loved one due to illness. She conducts bereavement groups and counsels individuals who have experienced losses. She also facilitates a support group for children whose parents have cancer or other serious illnesses.

She is trained in both crisis intervention and disaster mental health and responds to traumatic events in her role as a crisis team member for her school. As a former American Red Cross Disaster Mental Health Team Member, she was deployed to Mississippi during the aftermath of Hurricane Katrina, where she worked to console and to assist hundreds of victims who were grieving the loss of loved ones.

She resides in the South Hills of Pittsburgh, PA with her husband, Tony, and her son, Connor.

Made in the USA
Lexington, KY
07 May 2017